IOWA WOMEN'S
CORRECTIONS

IOWA WOMEN'S CORRECTIONS

A HISTORY

ERICA SPILLER

PEGGY LONG, CONTRIBUTOR

THE
History
PRESS

Published by The History Press
Charleston, SC
www.historypress.com

First published 2021

Manufactured in the United States

ISBN 9781467147255

Library of Congress Control Number: 2020948647

I think it is well understood that an institution is pitted against failure almost from the beginning. When the child comes into the institution they are confronted with that.... There is no doubt about it that any child, regardless of how well the job may have been done, will leave the institution with an institutional stigma because of the lack of education and understanding on the part of society as a whole. I hope there will come a day when institutions will not be needed. It is expensive. They do the best they can under the circumstances, but the job probably could be done just as well, and certainly far less expensively, if it could be done in a local community by the local probation workers and social workers and police force and churches and schools.

—Mrs. Marie Carter, superintendent of the Iowa Training Schools for Girls, 1954[1]

CONTENTS

ACKNOWLEDGEMENTS

This book was written over the course of eight years and finished at the height of a pandemic. It would never have reached completion without the support and ingenuity of many individuals along the way. The encouragement and compassion from so many people willing to help in preserving the historical record and supporting incarcerated individuals and the community was palpable and inspiring.

A tremendous debt of gratitude is owed to the amazing individuals working in state and national libraries, historical societies and museums for helping us acquire images while working primarily remotely during the COVID-19 pandemic. Even before the pandemic hit, many of them had already provided a warm welcome to roam their stacks of historical reports and documents.

Friends and family members deserve considerable thanks and praise for encouraging this work, even at times when the task seemed overwhelming or roadblocks appeared impassable. Their willingness to jump in and help with many tasks along the way, such as printing, scanning and uploading images and documents; providing feedback; or taking on more of the household responsibilities so time could be dedicated to this work, was invaluable.

Sincere gratefulness must also be offered to the incarcerated women and corrections employees for the welcome into their facility and for those who shared their stories. While personal stories of currently incarcerated individuals are not shared in this book, their experiences and reflections helped inform the scope and direction of this work. Thanks are given to those incarcerated women, staff and administrators in ensuring this facet of Iowa's history did not go unrecorded.

Much work has been done in an attempt to improve the state of women's corrections in Iowa, yet there remains significant work to do. Hopefully, this book will provide those interested in learning more about this area an easily accessible resource. Ideally, it will inspire action focused on making additional improvements to the state's correctional system for incarcerated women in which the women, their communities and their families will benefit.

THE HISTORY OF WOMEN'S PRISONS IN IOWA

When it was announced that the Iowa Correctional Institution for Women (ICIW) was about to undergo a major renovation, there was some excitement that Iowa's incarcerated women would have access to a new, state-of-the-art prison designed specifically with women's needs in mind. The original facility was homey, and it resembled a well-manicured, energetic college campus, nestled snuggly into the quaint town of Mitchellville, Iowa. Though the facility was as charming and comfortable as a prison can be, there were also buildings in need of repairs and updates to keep the facility safe and effective. Most of the buildings and infrastructure at the Mitchellville prison were the same ones designed to house juvenile girls decades earlier, and they were not well suited for the transition into a modern correctional facility.

The proposed and legislatively approved new women's facility would be located just down the hill on the west side of the initial site, prompting questions about which operations of the prison would continue to be housed in the former Girls Reform School buildings. Disappointingly, it turned out that the plan was to tear down most of the existing structures. In addition to demolishing the old facility, there was no plan for any historical documentation of the site that played such a large role in Iowa women's correctional history. The site started as Thomas Mitchell's high school and academy designed to prepare attendees for work or college, until the facility transitioned to its role as a state juvenile institution for young female Iowans, which it remained for most of its years. The site's final act was to serve as only the second correctional institution in the state of Iowa specifically designated for incarcerated adult women.

On learning that no official plans existed to document the historical significance of the original site and its structures, the idea for this book blossomed as an attempt to fill that gap. In the early stages of this work, it became clear that the original location at Mitchellville was not the only aspect of women's correctional history in the state that could fade from the narrative over time. In fact, other than scattered and occasional news articles, state reports and sporadic mentions in other books or documents, there seemed to exist no comprehensive history of the women's correctional system in Iowa. It was after this discovery that this book idea evolved to be inclusive of the entire history of women's corrections in Iowa and not exclusively the Mitchellville site.

The history collected here represents the sometimes limited and even possibly imprecise information that has remained to be found. For the first twenty years of the correctional system, Iowa was not even a state, and available documents detailing that time are scarce. Other than regularly filed biennial reports that superintendents and wardens were required to submit to the Iowa Board of Control, resources documenting the early years of women's corrections were often limited to newspaper stories, handwritten and typewritten internal notes and rulebooks and occasional firsthand accounts from incarcerated individuals, staff and family members. Great care has been taken to share the historical record as accurately as possible, given the state and quantity of the available information. If inaccuracies have occurred, they are entirely unintentional.

One particular circumstance in which some of the historical records were intentionally omitted in this work was when protecting the identities of incarcerated individuals or their victims. In many cases, the stories of certain incarcerated individuals and correctional employees are easily available through newspapers, official reports and other documents. However, stories included in this book are shared not to glorify crimes or to further demean or rebuke incarcerated individuals or staff but rather to provide a look with some additional texture and perspectives into the trends and conditions of the times.

As the system continued to evolve over time, so did the terminology used in Iowa's prisons. Efforts have been made to use correctional terms with respect to the era when discussing certain institutions. One particularly interesting set of terms that has changed over the centuries are the words that have been used to identify those housed in the facilities. At the beginning of the historical record, the incarcerated women and men were referred to as convicts. Over time, other titles were favored, including resident, client, inmate, offender and incarcerated individual. The titles of certain staff positions changed over the years, as well, such as guards evolving into correctional officers. The institution's leader was called the superintendent at women's prisons prior to the ultimate adoption of the current term, *warden*, a title not adopted for women until 150 years after it had been in use for male leaders at men's prisons. Beyond the terms used for people, language also changed as it referred to the units, buildings and institutions in which incarcerated individuals were housed. Terms such as *cottages*, *family homes*, *departments*, *work shops*, *cellblocks* and *units* were used to describe cell houses and rooms, and even institutions went through changes in names, such as *penitentiary*, *reformatory*, *industrial school*, *training school* and others. In many ways, the evolution of terminology helps display the sentiments and attitudes toward the correctional system, its goals and its inhabitants at a given time. When the focus was reformation and things seemed at their most cordial between staff and incarcerated individuals, the women were referred to as clients, and they lived in cottages. The environment was not always so friendly or homey, and the terms of a different time period were *inmate*, *unit* and *warden*.

The women's correctional system in the state has come a long way in its almost two-hundred-year history, but as will be shown, there exists a pattern of repeated situations throughout its history, some of which still occur in the present. Countless individuals have played many roles in the development of the correctional system. While there were certainly some troublesome figures along the way, both behind bars and holding the keys, there were many individuals who devoted their lives and attention to improving the situations and outcomes for those unfortunate enough to find themselves inside the walls of one of these facilities.

Correctional systems are influenced by a number of factors, including societal forces, legislative pressures, the criminality of drugs and alcohol, immigration trends, mental health, movements in reform and educational programs and many other variables. Simply put, corrections is an exceedingly broad topic, even when narrowed down to corrections focused on women in a particular state. With all of that in mind, this text simply aims to document the primary physical facilities that women were housed in throughout the history of Iowa. In doing so, trends and topics must be touched on to provide context or explanations for various events and circumstances. This is not to say that criminal justice reform is not necessary; it absolutely is, but that is a topic explored in many other texts. In this case, the aim is to document and preserve these historical facilities and the movement of incarcerated women throughout the state of Iowa as the state's correctional story was being written and up to the point where individuals are confined today. The final chapter on the state's current facility, the Iowa Correctional Institution for Women (ICIW), will provide a broad and brief overview of that facility. The technological era has provided an environment that makes vast amounts of information available about the current facility, including professional documentaries and in-depth news stories. Hopefully, the record of that facility will be better preserved in the historical record than the accounts of its predecessors.

To date, there have been six primary prisons or correctional facilities where women have been housed. Fort Madison and Anamosa were constructed for male prisoners, but they were the only penal institutions in the state at certain times to house women, since women did not have any facilities of their own. From there, the path diverged into juvenile and adult female facilities. Girls were first housed in the Girls Reform School in Salem, until their relocation to a facility in Mitchellville, Iowa. Adult women were transitioned from Anamosa to Rockwell City, the state's first all-female institution for adults, until they were sent to their current location in Mitchellville, Iowa, the site of the former Girls Reform School. Since their initial transition to the Iowa Correctional Institution for Women (ICIW) in Mitchellville, the original structures have closed, and ICIW broke ground on its new facility on adjacent land in 2010.

Girls and women have been housed in other locations for criminal offenses throughout Iowa's history, but the aforementioned institutions represent the major correctional facilities. Naturally, women have often been held in jails across the state; in various mental health facilities, such as Cherokee and Mount Pleasant; and other smaller juvenile sites, such as Good Shepherd Homes and the former juvenile facility in Toledo. While the jails, mental health facilities and juvenile facilities that housed smaller populations of women did play their part in the history of women's corrections, they fall outside the scope of this study focused on the larger, primary correctional institutions that held incarcerated women throughout the state. Although little of this text will be devoted to those facilities, it is important to note that by 2014 the last female juvenile facility in the state, Toledo, closed its doors by order of former governor Terry Branstad. Sentenced juvenile girls have since been sent out of state, even farther away from access to their families and community resources. By 2020, there were multiple facilities for juvenile boys and zero facilities able to take juvenile girls post-conviction. Almost as startlingly, the adult correctional system as of the same time period provides eight male prisons and one facility for women.

Some might suspect that the need for women's prisons is less than the need for male institutions, and to some extent, there is logic behind that sentiment. However, there are many reasons that despite the number of incarcerated women being far lower than the number of incarcerated men, the need for additional facilities and resources exists. As cited by many past correctional leaders, having few or ill-located facilities can limit community resources and work release opportunities, and it becomes more difficult for incarcerated individuals to have visitors or work to maintain relationships with their families and children.

The modern landscape of women's corrections demonstrates that despite many advances in the area, the state still has a long way to go. In some ways, there are even fewer services for women than there were over one hundred years ago. For nearly two centuries, since the first prison was established in Iowa, the state has continued to double back on its commitment to its incarcerated women and girls. Issues still remain, such as inadequate programming and education, lack of funding from the state and the need to address discrimination and social justice issues in the correctional system.

THE WOMEN'S PRISON SYSTEM in the state of Iowa has existed in many forms since the first women was documented as entering the system in the 1850s. In the years between then and now, women have experienced significant changes in their correctional environments. In some ways, it might seem like significant progress has been made for Iowa's incarcerated women, but in many ways, there remains a substantial amount of work to do. Women perpetually experienced inadequate and inequitable circumstances throughout the evolution of the prison system in Iowa, and there are many cases that exemplify that incarcerated women still face similar circumstances today.

The entire correctional system seems to be historically fraught with constant hurdles, such as insufficient government funding, overcrowding, lack of effective methods to further reduce recidivism, ample resources and training for incarcerated individuals aimed at successful reentry, complications of solitary confinement, incarceration of the mentally ill in prisons, racism and more. The women's system has not been immune to any of these and other hurdles, and in some cases, it has felt the burden at even greater levels. In the state of Iowa, incarcerated men had reformatory programs before similar services were offered to women. Women were prohibited from recreational opportunities in an effort to keep them out of sight of male inmates at one institution, and at another institution, they were denied most forms of recreation, as such activities were deemed unladylike. Lower numbers of imprisoned women resulted in educational programs being cut at certain times in Iowa's history and numerous calls for the single women's institution to be closed or relocated in an effort to make more room for incarcerated men.

The incarcerated women themselves were often an afterthought, as the female correctional system evolved, but they were not alone in the struggle. The prison staff also faced challenges not felt at the same levels by those in the men's systems. Female wardens were awarded lower salaries than their male counterparts at other facilities, even when faced with higher staffing ratios. Even men who worked at women's prisons were paid less than men working at male institutions. Beyond the differences in salaries, women also seemed to be assessed under a dissimilar set of parameters. Multiple news stories focused on the physical attractiveness or the marital and parental status of the leaders of women's facilities. While seemingly minor, disparities such as these demonstrate the deep social, cultural and political divisions and discrimination between the sexes, affecting the level of consideration and attention given to women.

Throughout the evolution of Iowa's female correctional system, numerous government officials, religious leaders, currently and formerly incarcerated individuals and private citizens worked hard to provide a safe and productive environment capable of helping the women to grow and successfully reenter society. That same goal continues to be shared by many today. This glimpse into the history of women's prisons in the state of Iowa might provide the opportunity to learn and reflect on this history and how the lessons it provides might help to continue improving the women's system in Iowa for those incarcerated, the employees who care for them, their families and the community.

1

FORT MADISON PENITENTIARY

The first half of the nineteenth century, the time in which the penitentiary at Fort Madison was erected, was a time of substantial growth and development in the area now known as Iowa. In a time of tumultuous relocations and skirmishes with Native Americans, in tandem with westward expansion, the soldiers in the area constructed the original Fort Madison, which was used as an early trading post and United States military fort. The fort, originally named Fort Bellevue, was built without the permission of indigenous groups and at a time when the expansion of the West was threatening Native American homelands and hunting grounds.[2] Siding with and oftentimes fueled by the British, Native American attacks on American forts became increasingly common, and Fort Madison was not immune. Fort Madison was attacked in 1812 and 1813 by a group of tribes, including Chief Black Hawk and the Sauk tribe, and by the end of 1813, the military would abandon the site after facing a shortage in provisions.[3] As the military abandoned the site, the original fort was burned down, but in the coming years, the city continued to develop around the area.

In the decades following the War of 1812, the United States government continued to work with the natives, sometimes through compromise and sometimes without, on establishing boundaries and acquiring land in the Iowa Territory. As the territory grew and the government claimed rights to a growing amount of land, non-natives began flooding into the state to make their homes and partake in the opportunities for mining and agriculture.[4] The population growth continued throughout the 1830s, and inhabitants

Fort Madison, United States military fort. *"The Iowa Forts,"* Annals of Iowa *4 (1899).*

of the Iowa Territory established communities and cities much like those of their neighbors to the east. Although the territory was not yet a state and the forms of local government were limited, a desire developed to protect society from those deemed a danger to it. To address the ever-growing calls for confinement of individuals convicted of crimes, in 1839, the City of Fort Madison built the first penitentiary for the soon-to-be state of Iowa.

Located a mile northeast of the former Fort Madison military outpost was Fort Madison, the penitentiary. Construction first began on the warden's mansion, which was a two-story stone building.[5] A building housing cells for the future convicts was also under construction; however, the inhabitants began arriving before any accommodations could be completed. In a rush, the convicts, as they were called at the time, dug a cellar beneath Warden Anderson's mansion, and the men were kept beneath the home until the cells were completed.[6] While the men were eventually moved to cells, the warden's home remained inhabited but by a new type of convict in the state's penal system: women.

State records were limited at the time, so it is unclear exactly who the first female convict was, when she arrived or for what reason she was incarcerated. The difficulty in discovering and understanding the early days of Iowa's first penitentiary might lie in the fact that Iowa was not even a state until seven years after the prison opened. After attaining statehood in 1846, it took almost another decade for the state legislature to establish committees and boards tasked with monitoring and reporting on state penal institutions.

In the mid-1850s, the first woman showed up in the records of Fort Madison, although limited attention is given to her reason for incarceration.[7]

Women were incarcerated at a much lower rate than men, and oftentimes, their crimes were not as violent. As a result, women frequently avoided long jail or prison stays, were fined as opposed to incarcerated or were immediately discharged.[8] It might be for these same reasons that the records and anecdotal stories of some of the earliest female convicts are absent or have been lost over time, or it might simply be the unfortunate trend that women are often not as well accounted for in recorded histories.

In the 1855 biennial report first mentioning women at Fort Madison, the warden wrote that no laws or policies had yet been enacted that would outline what was to be done with a woman convicted of a crime. In the instance of the first recorded female convict, the inspector on the case had required the warden of Fort Madison to take the woman into the warden's mansion where she would live among the family and be separated from the male convicts. Little else was mentioned about this one woman, except that she was in poor health.[9] In the following biennial report, one woman was again reported, and she was still living with the warden and his family. It is unclear whether this was the same or a different woman, but the warden reported this female convict was in good health.[10] Either the earlier woman had gotten better or a new woman had been sent to live with the warden. Although the report still featured little information about women, it had one additional fact when compared to the earlier reports. In the 1857 document, the warden stated that the one female convict was employed in making clothing for the incarcerated men. While the one woman was getting a bit more attention in the report, the document illustrated that provisions for dealing with incarcerated women still had yet to be developed.[11]

As the years passed, women received an increasing amount of attention from leaders at the penitentiary and state officials, although the states were often slower to respond to the growing demand for institutional resources and facilities for women. For almost two decades, the women were housed with the warden. Unlike the legislators tasked with funding the prison, the warden and other prison officials were concerned that the number of female convicts would likely continue to increase, and numerous calls were made to establish both policies and accommodations designed for the female prison population. In 1877, more than twenty years after the first female convict showed up in the records of Fort Madison, living quarters were finally developed solely to hold the women. Just as the first men at Fort Madison had been kept in the warden's mansion, the first female unit was also located in the warden's home, although this time, the upper story of the domicile was used. The second story of the house was officially

Warden's residence. *Personal collection of Erica Spiller.*

converted into two rooms designed to keep the female convicts separated from others. While this arrangement better suited the women and the penitentiary in the short term, the warden continued to vie for larger additional amenities for the still-growing female population.[12]

The two rooms for the women certainly signified an upgrade in the conditions and experiences of the female convicts; however, the close and crowded quarters resulted in the easy transmission of diseases and illnesses. Additionally, on at least one occasion, a child was born to a female convict who was allowed to keep her infant with her in the penitentiary.[13] To further exacerbate the crowded conditions, the women were frequently confined to their rooms in an attempt to limit their exposure to the male convicts. Continuing his cries for improvements, the warden urged state legislators to consider a paper written by Mrs. L.B. Benedict, in which the author championed the creation of a separate reformatory for women.[14] Lovina B. Benedict was an important figure in the reformation of women's prison rights of the time, and her efforts were echoed and supported by the Woman's Christian Temperance Union (WCTU), the group responsible for the creation of an all-female jail in Davenport, Iowa. Not only did Benedict cite the inappropriateness of housing women in the same cell blocks as men, but she also urged the state legislature to follow the successful model of the Women's Prison at Indianapolis, which had reported an 80 percent reform rate in the female population. Evident in Benedict's works was that the idea and treatment of the fallen woman was perpetuating the cycle of crime. Women convicted of offenses such as prostitution and keeping a house of ill-fame left jail and prison sentences destitute and with no means to make an honest living. In an effort to support themselves and survive, many female convicts had few options post-release beyond once again resorting to acts such as prostitution as a means for survival.[15] Aware of the lack of options for newly released convicts, Benedict and the WCTU championed reform and domestic training opportunities for incarcerated women so that female convicts would have a better chance at leading a productive and legal life after exiting a jail or penitentiary.

While calls for a separate female facility would continue to echo around the state, action would not be taken for some time and certainly not in time for some of Fort Madison's first well-documented convicts. Around the 1880s, clearer records of female convicts began to appear, and four of Fort Madison's women who entered the penitentiary were Lena Stanton, Anna Hower, Elizabeth Porter and Anna Taylor. Three of the women were convicted of murder, and one was incarcerated for larceny.

Lena Stanton, sent to Fort Madison in the 1880s, was convicted of larceny in Linn County. According to the *Graphic* and the *Chicago Daily Tribune*, Stanton came from a prominent family living in Keokuk, but

Shower line, Fort Madison yard. Some claim to see a woman in the foremost line. *State Historical Society of Iowa, Iowa City.*

she had chosen to deviate from her family's path. Stanton, a juvenile by today's standards, appeared to have a habit of thievery, and in 1881, she was sent to Fort Madison after stealing a horse and carriage. At her arrest, Stanton claimed she had stolen the carriage to help a friend get out of a situation in Keokuk.[16] Not only was Stanton merely seventeen at the time she committed her crime, but she was also with child. During the time she was held in the county jail, Stanton delivered the child. While in Fort Madison, now a young mother, Stanton soon found herself the fortunate recipient of an appeal for her release from a district judge and the penitentiary's chaplain. The chaplain claimed that Lena Stanton and her child had a caring and suitable home into which she could be released, and the governor granted her a conditional pardon.[17] Almost a decade later, another larceny was reported in Keokuk by a Lena Stanton, though it is unclear if it was the same woman as the accused horse thief. This time, the woman, employed as a domestic, stole a diamond from a house guest.[18] While Stanton was sent to Fort Madison for larceny, the three other known female convicts at the penitentiary were incarcerated for something far more serious.

Anna Hower was committed to Fort Madison in 1881 for poisoning her husband. According to the *Cedar Rapids Evening Gazette*, after poisoning her husband, Hower ran away with another man. On being caught, she claimed that the poisoning was an accident and that she thought she was giving her husband medicine.[19] For her crime, Hower received eighteen years,[20] but she was eventually transferred to another institution, from which she temporarily escaped and, for a brief period of time, roamed the streets in freedom by dressing as a man.[21]

The next woman, Elizabeth Porter, was also sentenced to prison for killing her husband, John Porter, but for very different reasons. Porter and her children had witnessed and put up with years of abuse committed by Elizabeth's husband, John Porter. According to author Kerry Segrave's recounting of the trial documents, the son of John and Elizabeth, also named John, returned to his home after quail hunting to find his father attacking his mother. John entered the physical altercation with his parents, and as John Porter Sr. was about to attack his wife with a club, he was shot by his son. The first shot did not stop the elder John, who turned to face his son. When he advanced, his son shot him again, killing him. Over a period of days, John concealed, moved, buried and ultimately staged his father's body to make it look like a suicide, but Elizabeth had told a neighbor what her son had done. Despite her alleged lack of involvement in the actual homicide, both Elizabeth and her son received twenty-one-year sentences to be served at Fort Madison Penitentiary.[22]

The third female convict sent to Fort Madison on murder charges in the 1880s was Mrs. Anna Taylor. Anna met a Mr. John S. Taylor, who eventually developed feelings for her, and Anna soon fell to liking John Taylor in return. However, John was already married when the two started to meet in secret. According to the *Eureka*, John's wife somehow limited his free time, which led John and Anna to develop a plot for murder. John and Anna allegedly poisoned the first Mrs. Taylor, and the day she was buried, the newly freed lovers married. The swiftness of their marriage aroused suspicion, and they were found guilty in 1883. Anna Taylor and her husband were sentenced to life in prison, of which Anna served only three years. After being transferred to a different penitentiary two years after her arrival at Fort Madison, Anna Taylor died of consumption. According to the *Eureka*, Anna was troublesome while in custody and was seriously bothered by the idea of being buried at the convicts' cemetery. She worked hard while incarcerated and managed to save enough money to buy a plot at a civilian cemetery, where she was buried after her death.[23]

Although some of the state's earliest-known female convicts were convicted of murder, throughout the years, the types of crimes women committed differed largely from those committed by men. While the disparity in criminal activity between men and women likely influenced the rates of incarceration and women's amenities in prison, the societal attitude toward women at the time also influenced the treatment of female criminals.

The crimes committed by women throughout the nineteenth century, particularly in the later part of the century, were most frequently crimes against public decency, including charges such as prostitution, keeping a house of ill-fame and lewdness. During the period, the women convicted of crimes involving sexual conduct often received the reputation of an outcast and were labeled "fallen women."[24] In the United States, as in Britain, fallen women were treated harshly by society, as these women were often perceived to threaten the ideal cultural norms and womanly roles they were to fulfill in the family unit. The unfavorable view of the women bled over into politics and corrections, and state officials often gave little care to the treatment of the women who were, in society's eyes, incapable of reform. When a woman was convicted of a crime and required to serve time, the nonviolent nature of their offenses usually kept them in jails as opposed to penitentiaries.[25] In fact, much later in the nineteenth century, over fifty years after Fort Madison became a penitentiary, a separate jail for women was established in the city of Davenport, Iowa, for the purpose of keeping the increasingly large number of female criminals separate from the men. The separate jailhouse helped prevent abuses and sexual assaults sometimes suffered by women held in the same facilities as men, and it provided women a female police matron who, it was thought, could better understand the female experience and perspective.[26] Unfortunately, such treatment of detained women in the Davenport jailhouse was too far in the future for the women committing crimes decades earlier, in the era of early Fort Madison.

Despite the gains made by the WCTU in procuring a women's jail and the acknowledgement of Benedict's plea by the legislature, the call for an official women's reformatory would not be answered for decades. Although there was little hope for improvements to be made at Fort Madison, slightly better accommodations for women were being developed at a new state penitentiary in Anamosa, Iowa. In 1883, three women were transferred to Anamosa from Fort Madison, and by 1897, any mention of women being held in Fort Madison disappeared from the biennial reports. While some women might have funneled through Fort Madison between 1883 and 1897, it seems they were quickly transferred to Anamosa, which was slightly more equipped to house female convicts.

While the female population was increasing at Anamosa and decreasing at Fort Madison, one noteworthy individual managed to make his way into Fort Madison. In 1891, Charles Miller, a "papa" with a child and wife, was sentenced to a two-year prison term in Fort Madison for horse stealing. For weeks, Charles worked in the shop repairing boots and bunked with his cellmate, Jacob Kraut. Shortly after his arrival, Miller fell ill and visited the doctor. Due to Miller's complaints of chest pain and sore lungs, the doctor requested the convict remove his shirt, but the doctor was met with Miller's refusal. Realizing that Charles Miller was not going to comply with the doctor's orders, the guard forcibly removed the convict's shirt, and Miller fainted and fell to the floor. The doctor was shocked to find that Charles Miller had been assigned female at birth. Little was known about Miller's life before or after prison, but it appeared that the convict was living as a man. Despite Miller's apparent wishes to live among men and be treated as one, the officials at Fort Madison provided Miller with women's clothes and shipped Charles to Anamosa to join the women housed there.[27]

In the late nineteenth century, over half a century after Fort Madison opened, the prison environment was starting to change for incarcerated women. As with most changes, though, improvements were slow and limited. The new jail in Davenport exemplified greater attention to the

Entry for Charles Miller in the Record of Convicts. A note says, "Transferred from Fort Madison." *State Historical Society of Iowa, Iowa City.*

increasing number of incarcerated women, as well as the differing needs of this population, and this same idea began to permeate the prison landscape. Beyond the jailhouse, small improvements were also being made for those serving prison sentences, and the newer state penitentiary in Anamosa was poised to offer women some amenities never seen before in the state of Iowa.

THE ADDITIONAL PENITENTIARY AT ANAMOSA

A s the population of Iowa grew, the number of incarcerated individuals continued to rise. The penitentiary at Fort Madison was no longer adequate to house the growing number of convicts, and its location in the far southeast corner of Iowa was not convenient for the rest of the state. Throughout the history of Iowa's correctional institutions, one recurring theme was the importance of location.

Fort Madison's location right along the Mississippi River provided convenient access to trade and water routes at the time of its construction. As the population expanded westward, the commission appointed with selecting a location for the new penitentiary looked for sites farther west. Beyond merely selecting a place more conveniently located, the commission and legislature also sought a site that would prove financially useful. In an effort to defray the expenses associated with building an additional prison, the legislature approved a location situated at a rock quarry in Anamosa, Iowa, in 1872.[28] The intent was for convict labor to be used in building the new penitentiary, but temporary cells had to be erected before any prisoners could be transferred for this purpose. To prepare the location to receive convicts, a small building containing wooden cells and a tall stockade wall were erected using hired labor.[29] On May 13, 1873, twenty male convicts were transferred from Fort Madison to begin construction on the first cell block. The first permanent structure, Work Shop No. 1, included a dining room, chapel, library and hospital, in addition to the cells.[30] By 1875, construction was finished on at least one cell house, and work had begun on

Convict labor being used to build the new penitentiary at the quarry in Anamosa, Iowa.
State Historical Society of Iowa, Iowa City.

a second. About a year after the construction was finished on the original permanent housing unit, the first record pertaining to a woman appears in the biennial report submitted to the legislature.[31]

While the biennial report for 1875–77 shows a woman present in the convict population, there is no mention of her elsewhere throughout the report. In contrast to the one woman housed in the Additional Penitentiary at Anamosa during this period, there were 284 men.[32] The same occurrence is noted in the following biennial report spanning the years of 1877 to 1879. In this case, a woman is again tallied in the quantity of convicts; however, her name, crime or any other information about her incarceration is omitted.

While the female population remained stable during this new biennial period, the male population had increased to 454 convicts.[33] The first substantial mention of the female population appears in the biennial report of 1879–81, in which A.E. Martin, Anamosa's second warden, recommends a separate prison be established for the incarceration of women.[34]

Although the earliest biennial reports of the Additional Penitentiary did not list much information about the women, two clerks, under the direction of Warden McClaughry in 1915, were asked to compile a complete listing of all the prisoners who had been held in Anamosa between 1873 and 1915. While some names are limited to first initials, making it difficult to identify the genders of convicts, some of the names and crimes of the earliest women do appear. Based on the records compiled by Warden McClaughry's clerks, it appears that one of the first female convicts housed in the penitentiary in Anamosa was Louisa Miller, who was received in 1876 for larceny and sentenced to a term of one year.[35] Fifteen days before completing her sentence, the acting governor, Samuel J. Kirkwood, pardoned Miller, and she was released from prison.[36]

More information is available about another early Anamosa woman, Lillian Merchant, who was committed to the institution on December 2, 1878.[37] Merchant, found guilty of adultery, exemplified a growing trend in women's incarceration in county jails and prisons in the state. While men were most commonly convicted and committed for crimes involving violence, theft and other acts against persons or property, women continued to be swept into the correctional system at a higher rate than men for crimes against public decency.

By 1881, the number of female convicts had grown from one to four, but during the earliest years of the Additional Penitentiary at Anamosa, it is unknown precisely where women were kept in the institution. It is not until the report of 1881–83 that the situation of women in the prison becomes clearer. In 1883, the three female convicts transferred from Fort Madison were added to the population already at Anamosa, which brought the total number of women kept during the biennial period to twelve. Despite the pleas for a separate women's facility by both the warden and the architect, no such amenities had been constructed, and the women were kept in Work Shop No. 1. A matron, Mrs. E.J. Wood, was hired to manage the women's unit,[38] and from that point forward, the female convicts slowly and sometimes painfully gained more attention from prison officials and state legislators.

Although the women were making small gains in prisons, many of the incarcerated women at the turn of the twentieth century might have been

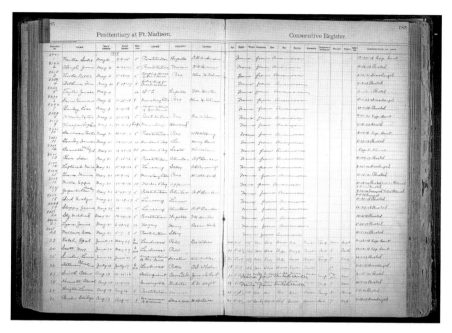

A section of the Consecutive Registers showing common offenses of incarcerated women. *State Historical Society of Iowa, Iowa City.*

less likely to even see the inside of a cell in today's legal system. One of Anamosa Penitentiary's most notorious female convicts, Margaret Hossack, was sentenced to life for killing her husband (a sentence that would later be overturned by the Iowa Supreme Court). It was a different time for women compared to today's standards, and Hossack was pressured by neighbors to not share her concerns regarding her husband's bad behavior and threats lodged at her and her children. In 1900, Hossack was accused of reaching her limit with her husband's tantrums, and the prosecutor alleged that she killed him with multiple axe strikes to the head. Despite the well-known abuses suffered by Hossack and her children, the court at the time did not see her actions as any sort of self-defense, and Margaret Hossack was charged with first-degree murder. The abuse by her husband was used as motive to convict her of first-degree murder in contrast with today's possible application as an appeal for a lesser charge or a self-defense plea.[39]

Despite the all-male jury's insistence that John Hossack's abuse was evidence and motive for murder, some prison officials and legislators were starting to notice that murder was not always a premeditated act of malice but instead sometimes a situational reaction to a set of unfortunate or impossible conditions. The court of public opinion toward Margaret Hossack began to shift, and many even blamed themselves for not doing more to help with her challenging home life. In Hossack's case, the Supreme Court of Iowa overturned her life sentence due to concerns regarding procedural issues in the original trial. Another trial was held following the Supreme Court's decision, but the jury could not reach a unanimous decision, and Hossack was freed.[40]

Margaret Hossack, deemed by some as the "Lizzie Borden of Iowa," drew a lot of attention from the press and citizens for multiple reasons. First, the grizzly nature of the crime and the trial surrounding it stirred up interest in the local community and the state. But perhaps more importantly, the question of domestic abuse playing a role in murder not only struck a chord with some attorneys, corrections officials and many citizens, it also caught the attention of the press and authors. The Hossack case inspired the popular Susan Glaspell one-act, *Trifles*, and her short story, "A Jury of her Peers." Glaspell was one of the reporters who covered the crime and trial, and the Hossack case inspired her to craft multiple literary pieces containing themes similar to those encountered in Margaret Hossack's life and trial.[41]

Although her case was quite notorious, Margaret Hossack was not the first woman sent to Anamosa for allegedly harming a family member. Additionally, the Anamosa to which Hossack was sentenced in 1901 was about to become more comfortable and accommodating to women than the facility available to those who came a couple decades earlier. Almost twenty years before Hossack arrived at Anamosa, a mother and her daughters were incarcerated for killing their father. The Lenihan women, Anna, Maggie and Anna (Annie), had confessed to killing John Lenihan, reported as an abusive husband. According to the Grundy County Historical Museum, John Lenihan appeared to have been shot through the window by an unknown assailant. On further investigation, a letter was found in which the younger Anna Lenihan, then seventeen-years-old, wrote that her father had thrown a cup of hot tea in mother Anna Lenihan's face. In the letter, Anna mentioned that her sister, Maggie, said that if the father continued to be abusive he would need to be shot, and Maggie was willing to do it. After the letter was revealed, young Anna confessed to the women's roles in the murder. The three had apparently been planning the murder for months, and Maggie finally killed her father with a gunshot to the head. John Lenihan had been reading in front of a window in the living room, and it was from inside that room that he was shot. To shield themselves from discovery, the Lenihan girls went outside and broke the glass in the window from the exterior. However, their plan for deception did not pan out, and the women were found guilty of second-degree murder.

The older Anna Lenihan and her daughter Maggie were sentenced to life in prison, while seventeen-year-old Anna received ten years.[42] On their arrival at Anamosa in December 1882, the women found themselves housed in Work Shop No. 1 under the purview of Matron E.J. Wood. Women incarcerated in Anamosa during the prison's earliest years had few options for activities, education or even simple mobility throughout the institution. In an effort to keep women safe, and in accordance with the decorum of the times, the male and female populations were kept separate. The isolation of female convicts left them in close quarters with little exercise or stimulation. One of the few activities in which the women engaged included mending the clothing and bedding for the institution. The warden and matron were aware of the direness of the situation and continued to request a separate women's prison from state legislators.[43] While numerous calls for improvement were being made, it would be long after the Lenihan women's departures that significant changes would take place.

The youngest Lenihan received a governor's pardon in 1884 and was released from Anamosa before any significant changes were made to the women's department. The older Lenihans, Anna and Maggie, were pardoned a couple years later, in 1886.[44] By the time the women were released, Anamosa was on its way to improving the living conditions of its female convicts. By the printing of the eighth biennial report, in 1887, a new women's facility was under construction on the grounds of the Additional Penitentiary at Anamosa.

While the future female department was under construction at the Additional Penitentiary, a new ward to house the mentally ill was completed. When women were next moved into a better situation, it was only a slight improvement. From their previous close quarters in Work Shop No. 1, the women were moved into one ward of the new insane department. Although the move to the insane department provided temporary relief, it, too, became overcrowded, and the women's options and mobility were still limited by their proximity to male convicts. One of the few improvements for women was that they had more work tasks available to them. While housed in the insane ward, the women were tasked with sewing, cleaning and doing laundry. Unfortunately, they did not receive the same recreational and educational opportunities as the men. They occasionally had teachers or lessons, but the fluctuating population and firm rule that they be separated from contact and out of sight of male convicts kept opportunities limited.[45]

By 1900, the female wing was officially finished, yet women would not be transferred into that section of the facility for another two years. Although the women were not yet in their new facility, they were receiving more attention around the turn of the century. A matron's report was included with each biennial report, and more focus was placed on the operations of the department and success of female convicts. From the matron's report, a clearer picture of the female population began to develop.

The population tended to stay around twenty female convicts. The notably low number of women could have been due to the propensity at the time to house woman in county jails or evidence of the nature of their crimes. In 1900, 50 percent of the women housed at Anamosa were incarcerated for crimes against public decency, including adultery, keeping a house of ill-fame, resorting to a house of ill-fame, prostitution and violation of liquor laws. In contrast, only 19 percent of Anamosa's male convicts were incarcerated for similar crimes.[46] The crimes committed by women tended to be nonviolent, and many of the women admitted to the penitentiary in the early twentieth century did not have any prior convictions. Further demographic information recorded around the time indicates that about three quarters of the women were White, most were married or widowed and the majority claimed to not use drugs, tobacco or alcohol.[47] In the 1901 to 1903 biennial report, the warden also mentioned that none of the women incarcerated were insane, and as a result, he deduced that women were mentally stronger than men.[48]

The Insane Department, where women were temporarily housed. *State Historical Society of Iowa, Iowa City.*

The finished Female Department at Anamosa, completed in 1900. *State Library of Iowa.*

Though women might have been primarily sentenced for crimes against public decency, some women, like Hossack and the Lenihan women, were sentenced for more violent crimes. In 1901, Lucy Foster was sentenced to three years for assault with the intent to murder. The victim, her husband, later requested her parole on his own account that he could not handle the children alone. Foster's parole was granted by the governor so that she might return home to care for the children.[49] The Foster case exemplifies yet another difference in the treatment of the sexes in prison and in society. In concert with the disparate treatment of the sexes, it was over six decades after the founding of the initial Iowa prison for men before women would have their first official housing unit in a state-run penitentiary.

Finally, in February 1902, nearly half a century after women appear in the state's prison record, the approximately twenty women housed in Anamosa were moved into their own Female Department in the institution.[50] For a few more years, the number of female convicts continued to fluctuate, and a temporary dip in numbers caused schooling to be discontinued, even though the women had their own department. However, around 1910, the population began a fairly steady climb upward, and by 1912, the population had almost doubled to forty-two women.[51] Aside from shifts in the population and relocation to their own housing facility, women also witnessed another change in the institution when it was turned into a men's reformatory.

The country had been swept up by a prison reform movement aimed at improving convicts as opposed to merely incarcerating them. In 1907, the State Penitentiary at Anamosa was renamed the Iowa State Reformatory, and the institution modeled its practices after the first reformatory, the Elmira Reformatory, which had opened in 1876 in New York. The reformatory was intended for male prisoners between the ages of sixteen and thirty who were deemed capable of transformation. Under this new mandate, Warden McClaughry argued that the female and mentally ill populations at the facility needed to be removed to meet the goals of the reform movement. He stated that the presence of women at the facility was "hurtful in the extreme" to the goal of reform and that the "criminally ill" needed to be removed, as they were thought to be incapable of reform.[52]

While the reform movement was popular, it only extended as far as male prisoners at Anamosa. As a result, the warden also insisted in the 1911 to 1912 biennial report that a new, completely separate facility must be made for women. In his eyes, it was not fair to the women that they did not have the same opportunity for reform as their male counterparts did at the Iowa State Reformatory.[53] While men were being reformed and enjoying the yard and other institutional facilities, opportunities for recreation and moving throughout the facility were still off limits to women as they were stifled by the large male population.[54]

Eventually, the frequent cries for a dedicated space for women were heeded. It took over twenty-five years for women to get their own housing facility since relocating to Anamosa, yet it took only six more years for the prison to remove them from the facility completely. A new, women's-only facility was opened in Rockwell City, Iowa, in 1918, and on May 21 of the same year, the women at Anamosa were transferred to the new facility.[55] Following the transfer of women to Rockwell City, there would be one final large incarceration of women at Anamosa. The Iowa State Reformatory at Anamosa held fifty-six women for the United States government for a little over a year, until the remaining female convicts were also transferred to Rockwell City.[56] After the remaining women were transferred, the part of the facility formerly known as the Female Department was used as sleeping quarters during surges in the male convict population.[57]

3

GIRLS REFORM SCHOOL AT MITCHELLVILLE

The topic of women's corrections is expansive, and many areas, such as juvenile detention and services for mentally ill women, helped shaped the landscape into what it is today. Although the facilities for juveniles and individuals with mental illnesses had a significant influence on the development of Iowa's correctional systems for women, the depth of their contributions cannot be captured under the limited topic of adult women's prisons. To attempt to fully chronicle the many institutions that held convicted women of all ages and conditions would not give adequate attention that incarcerated women of all types, and those who help them, deserve. However, to understand the current state of women's prisons in Iowa, one juvenile facility that played a significant role in the system's evolution must be explored. The former Girls Reform School was primarily located on the current grounds of the Iowa Correctional Institution for Women (ICIW) in Mitchellville. Not only were the grounds of the juvenile facility the same as the first ICIW facility, but also the beginning of the Girls School in many ways paralleled the evolution of women's corrections at Fort Madison and Anamosa.

The Girls Reform School ultimately made its permanent home in Mitchellville, but White's Manual Labor Institute, the institution that first housed the juvenile corrections movement, was originally located in Salem, Iowa. The path to establishing the first juvenile facility for women was a bumpy one and began in earnest in January 1868, when Governor Samuel Merrill addressed the need for a juvenile reform school in his inaugural

Entryway to the Girls Reform School. *State Historical Society of Iowa, Iowa City.*

ceremony. At the time, there was a pervasive belief in environmentalism as the influencing factor of those committing "evil" acts. Religious leaders, politicians and community members predominantly felt that young people who committed unacceptable acts were doing so as a result of their environmental conditions. The theory advanced by many officials and citizens was that if these juveniles could simply be removed from urban centers, abusive homes, homes with absent parents or environments with limited supervision or morals, then the state could reform them into proper and productive citizens. Such an idea was already popular on the East Coast, in London and, in particular, with members of the Quaker community. In Lancaster, Massachusetts, an Industrial School for Girls had been established based on the philosophy of Charles Loring Brace, who felt that juvenile girls needed a family environment away from urban settings, where a rural and agrarian life could be led. After the Lancaster School, the first reform school in Iowa became the second school of its type in the entire nation.[58]

Iowa's focus on reform was propelled by the state's three-tiered approach to supporting its troubled citizens throughout the years of 1838 to 1860. Initially, members of society who needed assistance, such as those struggling with mental or physical disabilities, the elderly and the poor, were assisted by casual systems of support, such as those offered by local churches or community members. Eventually, people in such conditions began to gain the attention of politicians who started writing laws to address support or treatment of such individuals, as well as addressing concerns related to violations of public morals. The 1838–39 legislature passed a bill to define how those deemed "insane" would be treated. It is important to note at that time insanity was not a medical term but a legal one. A person's insanity was decided by a jury of twelve men who did not necessarily include doctors, and those under judgment could include "every idiot, non-compos, lunatic, and distracted person."[59] Then, in 1851, the legislature adopted laws against those engaged in vagrancy, defined as fortunetellers, drunks, prostitutes and people "having no visible calling or business to maintain themselves." This same legislation made other acts illegal, including adultery, operating a house of ill-fame, recruiting someone to work at a house of ill-fame and sharing any "obscene book, picture, or song that tended to corrupt the morals of the young." In fact, much of the legislation specifically mentioned the protection of the state's younger citizens.[60]

With many new laws established and a focus on protecting youth, in 1860, the state began reallocating its funds toward constructing and financing its own statewide charitable institutions instead of continuing to funnel money into local organizations. Shortly thereafter, and with encouragement from Governor Merrill's speech, two congressmen began drawing up plans for the establishment of the state's first reform institution for juveniles. Representatives Douglas Hard of Lee County and Thomas Dudley of Henry County brought forth Solferino Farms in Lee County and White's Manual Labor Institute in Henry County for consideration as possible sites.[61]

Ultimately, state leaders felt that Solferino Farms, near Keokuk, was too close to other villages and towns, which they felt might have a criminal element and could be too enticing to young people. It was also determined that the land was not as high of quality, which could result in lower revenues than would be necessary to sustain the school. White's Manual Labor in Salem, Iowa, had much higher-quality land, and it was farther away from any villages or towns than Solferino Farms. While the location was preferred, one of the complications was that the land and buildings would need to be leased.[62]

Josiah White, a Quaker, member of the Society of Friends and the founder of Lehigh Coal and Navigation Company, wanted to start a training school where children could receive a religious education in line with White's beliefs. In 1851, White passed away, but he left behind $20,000 to build White's Manual Labor, intended as a school for poor children, "white, colored, and Indian."[63] The Iowa Yearly Meeting of Friends was not developed enough to take on the task, so in 1864, the Indiana Yearly Meeting of Friends purchased the land, appointed a board and selected a president so the school could become a reality. Despite the best intentions of White and the initial board, funds were scarce, and it took the appointment of a new board (over a decade later) to secure enough money for the first physical building to be erected. By 1868, all of the funds had been used, and the project was $2,000 in debt. Farming at the site was bringing in $1,500 in revenue, but the trustees did not feel the sum was enough to successfully run the institution. When White left the money for the facility, he had stipulated that the site could not be used for profit or sold. This left the trustees in a difficult situation.

Coincidentally, the institute's money began to wane during the same time frame that the state was in search of a site to house the new reform school. The trustees, perhaps due to Representative Dudley, offered to lease the facility to the state. The land at White's was of high quality and was good for farming, and the institution was far enough away from villages and towns that state leaders found it to be a suitable location for the future juvenile reform school. The motion was approved and passed into law by the legislature on March 31, 1868, and by October 7, the first male juvenile was committed to the reform school in Salem, Iowa.[64]

The superintendent of the Reform School, Joseph McCarty, reported that in the first year of its operation, the school had received forty-six juveniles between the ages of nine and eighteen years old, only one of whom was a girl. For lack of space, she was housed with the superintendent's family. Although the legislative language seems to imply that boys or girls could use the facility, few girls were ever admitted, until 1873. The boys who were admitted to the facility from 1868 to 1873 were primarily committed for reasons such as larceny, vagrancy, incorrigibility and burglary. In addition to listing the reasons for admittance, the superintendent echoed the sentiments of the environmentalist movement, noting that many of the boys came from families lacking either a mother, father or both due to death, and some boys also came from homes where the parents were separated.[65]

A few years after the reform school received its first juvenile, the legislature and other officials started lamenting the fact that the school grew rapidly overcrowded, and access to the school, due to its location, was inconvenient. The superintendent also added that the capacity and lack of a separate building prohibited access to women.[66] McCarty reproached the fact that the first woman to be admitted to the institution had to be housed with his family. He felt a separate facility was necessary, though he stated that having the girl stay with his family was "not very bad."[67] By 1872, all of the four girls who had been committed to the reform school were housed with McCarty's family. Each girl was treated in much the same manner as his children and were not subjected to the discipline of the school. Given the conditions and lack of adequate facilities, girls were released as soon as possible, and the superintendent fully admonished the legislature for its failure to address the situation.[68] While McCarty was displeased with the legislature's lack of attention to juvenile girls, he should not have been surprised. It was fewer than two decades before when the first adult woman had to be housed in the warden's home at Fort Madison Penitentiary due to a lack of women's accommodations in that correctional facility.

Without the level of legislative support that McCarty felt was appropriate, he began pushing back by refusing to accept new commitments to the school. Additionally, the trustees argued that the positive results of the school were worth more funding from the state. The line of logic they used was that it cost $600 per annum to care for the committed juveniles. Of the 136 boys who had come through the school, roughly 75 percent of them, or 102 boys, were reformed and living as productive citizens. As a result, the trustees posited that the state could expect financial returns far exceeding their initial investment and should invest more to yield even higher dividends. It was also made clear to the general assembly that the high rate of incarceration of boys was leaving little room for them to house girls separately. Perhaps in response to this pressure from the Reform School, in 1872, the legislature "ordered" the school to receive girls, and a tenant house was quickly converted for this purpose. Additionally, the general assembly continued to push that the facility accommodate both sexes, yet they ordered that boys and girls be completely separated and unable to communicate with each other. Despite that order, in November 1872, McCarty was running out of space in the newly converted tenant house, and he felt that he could not properly supervise the female adolescents when they were not housed in the same building. Against the direction of the legislature, McCarty moved the girls back into the same building as the boys, and the six girls occupied the top floor of the main building, while the boys were housed on the bottom floor. Whether or not it was the result of McCarty's protest is debatable, but soon after his desegregation of the sexes, the legislature once again cited concerns about the sexes being housed together and decided to relocate the juvenile boys to a new location.[69]

Portrait of L.D. Lewelling.
Photograph Collection, Board of Regents; Individuals, record series no. 23, University Archives, Rod Library, University of Northern Iowa.

The early 1870s brought big changes for corrections in Iowa. The site for the Additional Penitentiary at Anamosa was secured in 1872, and a short time later, juvenile boys were transferred from the facility in Salem, Iowa, to the still-used juvenile institution in Eldora, Iowa. Around the same period, leaders at the Girls Reform School in Salem began requesting a permanent location, as opposed to their leased facility at the former White's Manual Labor site.

On April 1, 1873, the reform school for girls officially opened, and two Quakers, Lorenzo D. Lewelling and his wife, Angeline, were appointed the superintendent and matron.[70] When Lorenzo and Angeline took control of the facility for girls, they first had only six young women under their immediate charge. Throughout the first year of the school's girls-only status (although boys would periodically be held prior to transfer to Eldora), fewer than a dozen women were in the facility at any given time.[71] The population of female juveniles in confinement was growing but certainly not at the rate of men being sent to the still infantile system of juvenile corrections.

The disparity in the incarceration rate between men and women was influenced by the difference in the criminal offenses of the sexes and how boys and girls were viewed in society. While girls were also incarcerated for crimes such as larceny, vagrancy and incorrigibility, they were more likely than men to be accused of additional crimes against public decency, such as prostitution or immoral conduct. When accused of a crime of an immoral or sexual nature, young girls were often sent by local authorities or family members to religious or private reform-type institutions, such as Good Shepherd Homes. In fact, police matron Sarah Hill in Davenport, Iowa, rarely sent any girls to state-run facilities, unless she was required to due to a criminal conviction or a parent or guardian petitioning an official declaration of incorrigibility. Instead, Matron Hill worked with parents and authorities to send young women to Good Shepherd Homes, which offered more extralegal flexibility in teaching, or controlling, girls who were known to have committed or were thought to be at risk for committing crimes of a sexual nature. It is important to note that the juvenile justice system was still in its infancy, and many jurisdictions and court systems placed juveniles in various facilities as they saw fit, even if the decision did not technically comply with state laws.[72]

Conclusions could be drawn that the low number of women in confinement resulted in the lack of funding based on need, and that might be true in part; however, that historical lack of appropriations and lodgings for women and girls paints a picture of a legislature that consistently funded correctional facilities for men at a rate that outpaced the needs of the growing female prison population.

Not only was the disparity between the sexes evident in the funds the legislature allocated to facilities but also in the pay of the superintendents and matrons, which varied significantly. In 1875, the combined pay of the superintendent and matron at the boys department was $1,500, while the salary for the two leaders at the girls department totaled $900. Furthermore, the boys department had twenty-two staff members, and the girls department had four. An initial instinct might be to explain the disparities in pay and staffing with the inmate population at each facility, but there were 135 boys in Eldora at the time and 30 girls in Salem. Based on the population total, the male facility had a 1:6.1 staff-to-juvenile ratio, and the female facility had a 1:7.5 staff-to-juvenile ratio. Despite the limited staffing and funding at the girls school, the superintendent noted in his biennial report that all of the girls who had been released so far, except for three whose whereabouts were unknown, were doing well, and one was even putting herself through college.[73]

From 1873 to 1875, forty-seven young women came through the girls school, and 60 percent were sent to the facility for incorrigibility or vagrancy. The nonviolent nature of these common crimes might have accounted for the numerous reports of success with girls who had been released. Crimes against morality, such as prostitution and immoral conduct, accounted for 23 percent of the offenses that landed a juvenile female in the facility. Finally, the third most common offenses, those against people or property, such as larceny and manslaughter, only accounted for 15 percent of crimes committed by girls sent to the school during the period.[74]

For the next few years, the facility in Salem continued with relative normalcy. The population increased slightly year over year, but the department was relatively free of problems from the juveniles. The school did not use restraints or have fences. Despite the lax security, only one escape by two girls occurred between 1875 and 1877. The girls were divided into two grade levels, and half of the day was spent in school, while the other half was spent learning manufacturing trades or household industries. The girls played a large role in the sustainability and operation of the facility by doing much of the grounds work, tending to livestock, mending clothes and completing housework in the living spaces. Despite the success of the institution, the facility was once again running out of space for the growing population, and the same accessibility issues that plagued those traveling to the once-male facility still affected the girls needing to be transported to and from Salem.[75] So, when the lease on White's expired in 1878, the girls department was temporarily relocated to a newly leased facility one mile west of Mount Pleasant.[76]

Before the short-term relocation to Mount Pleasant, and with an interest in cost savings, the general assembly again considered housing both sexes together and sending the girls to the facility for boys in Eldora. A number of people, including the Lewellings and the superintendent of the Cincinnati House of Refuge, had serious concerns about housing boys and girls in Eldora, which they expressed to the legislature. A joint committee of the general assembly was sent to visit the school and ultimately agreed that the girls should have their own facility and not be required to share a school with boys.[77]

Following the temporary relocation of the school to Mount Pleasant, the number of incarcerated women continued to climb. After the move, the population grew rapidly by 40 percent. Over sixty girls were being housed in one room that measured thirty by forty feet and had an eight-foot-tall ceiling. The kitchen was twelve by sixteen feet and proved inadequate for preparing the necessary amount of food.[78] Despite the increase, 75 percent of girls released from the facility were considered reformed. Many of the former girls even stayed in touch with Mrs. Lewelling after their departure. In one letter, a former resident wrote:

My Dear Mrs. Lewelling:

I almost wish I were back going to school again, but I have plenty to do to employ my mind. I have a sweet little babe one year old; have been married three years in June. Pa just thinks the world of my husband. I am talking of going home on a visit; but this time would rather come and see you—shall I come? Now write me a good long letter and tell all about the school. With love to all, I am,

Yours, - -

Another former resident of the institution wrote the following to Mrs. Lewelling:

> *My Dear Mrs. Lewelling:*
> *I received your kind letter; was so glad to hear from you. We have moved to our new home. The house has five rooms in it. We have a large lot—are all the time improving it. I am as happy as I can be and don't think any girl in the world, rich or poor, can get a better husband than I have.*

Many correspondences flowed in and reported that the girls were doing well and seemed to have enjoyed, and even missed, the time they spent in the girls department.

In addition to sharing correspondences in the biennial publications, follow-up reports were included for many girls who had left the institution. A few of the reports included:

> *No. 18, committed, November, 1873; larceny. Discharged, 1876. Married; living in Chicago; husband a pilot on a lake vessel.*
> *No. 36, committed 1875; incorrigibility. Discharged, 1878. Does laundry work in the city of Des Moines; well respected.*
> *No. 75, committed, August, 1877, for—. Discharged, 1879. Since married; both her husband and herself have good positions in a State institution.*[79]

The anecdotal successes and shared correspondences from the time helped add color to the success metrics that the institution had reported.

While the girls department was functioning well despite its challenges in Mount Pleasant, a familiar trend to what had occurred with White's Manual Labor Institute was brewing in Mitchellville, Iowa. Another citizen of Iowa and founder of the city of Mitchellville, Thomas Mitchell, had built and was operating a religious institution for instruction called the Universality Seminary. After some time, Mitchell had not been able to pay off the debt caused by establishing the seminary, and it looked as though Mitchell's school would need to close.[80] Around the same time period, the general assembly began to accept that it would be best to cease renting spaces for the Girls Reform School and started to search for a site that it could purchase. The trustees of Mitchell Seminary contacted the legislature and offered to sell the property for $20,000. As the seminary was designed as a school, it suited the needs of the reform school well, and the trustees even offered to include a

Mitchell Seminary.
*State Historical Society
of Iowa, Iowa City.*

number of furniture pieces and supplies in the sale of Mitchell's Seminary. The state ultimately accepted the offer to purchase the seminary, and in 1880, the Girls Reform School at Mitchellville opened.[81]

The girls department in Mitchellville remained under the daily management of Mrs. Lewelling, while Mr. Lewelling still led the operation and oversight of the facility. The new facility consisted of a brick building that had two stories and a basement. In addition, the property featured a barn, a laundry and forty acres of land. By 1881, there were only sixty-three girls at the school, but due to the still inadequate housing, the girls had to sleep eight to a room designed for two. Just as women in Anamosa had to deal with complications during their periods of close quarters, the inadequate housing space might have caused some of the illnesses that spread through the girls department. The first casualty that occurred on the premises was "Little Mollie," identified in the report as "an interesting little colored girl," who died of scrofula, or tuberculosis, on January 28, 1881. Little Mollie was the first girl "laid to rest in a corner of our own farm."[82] It is likely that Little Mollie was buried in what has been rediscovered as a small cemetery located at the southwest corner of the property. While there is no tombstone with the name of Mollie on it, there is a stone with the same death date as Mollie's marked "Mary Clark." While a few names remain discernable on some of the markers, only one appears to have been officially filed with the county records department.[83] The available records and markers leave few clues about how the girls died, but sickness occasionally struck in the institution.

Cramped living conditions and threats of illness were real, but they were not enough to impede progress at the school. Mrs. Lewelling and her supporters pushed back against many obstacles thrown at them, which also sometimes included the public's perception of such a facility. In her 1881 report on the state of the girls department, Matron Lewelling stated, "We are aware that there is some scepticism [sic] in regard to the reformation of girls, but it is without reason, and arises from ignorance and prejudice." Lewelling's confidence in her efforts and the ability to reform girls paid off, as she was met with great results.[84] Mr. Lewelling also adamantly defended the success of the school in both the 1880 and 1882 reports he filed with the legislature, citing that roughly 70 to 75 percent of the girls were successfully reformed, an account verified by correspondence and reports from formerly incarcerated girls. It seemed that the efforts of the Lewellings were recognized when the 1882 general assembly's visiting committee reported that the girls at the Reform School were performing higher academically than their peers attending public school. The report from the committee also included praise for the programming provided at the school, such as gymnastics, singing, marching and rhetorical exercises.[85]

Part of the success at the Girls Reform School was attributed to Superintendent Lewelling's "three phased system of education." The goal, Lewelling thought, was for the girls to strive toward personal virtue, which could be accomplished through common schooling, mastery of the domestic sciences and religious instruction.

Unless a girl had reached the age of majority, which at the time was eighteen years old, she would be held in the reformatory school until she had proven she could cook, do laundry and sew.[86] According to Superintendent Lewelling, "No girl is permitted to leave the institution until she has become proficient in every department of household work. In other words, she must work in the kitchen until she can cook a good dinner without help. She must work in the laundry until she can wash and iron well; in the sewing room until she can do neat work with the needle."[87]

The reform school helped develop domestic skills in young women to better situate them for their own adult home life and to improve the odds of being able to place girls post release with families needing domestic help. In fact, the school was so successful at training and placing the girls that the applications from citizens requesting help exceeded the number of available girls.[88]

The commitment to placing girls in industrial positions was so great that in 1886, the name was changed from the stigma-laden reformatory school to the Girls Industrial School of Iowa. Despite the transition, the school was still intended to feel more like a home than a penal institution. Representative R.S. Finkbine stated, "Our Institution is not a penal institution, but a home, in every sense the word implies, for the wards of the State." The one building in which the girls were housed was called the family building or family home,[89] and girls enjoyed many activities in addition to their schooling, including music and outdoor activities.

In addition to the emphasis the school placed on domestic sciences, common schooling and religion were also considered important. A general opinion existed that young women who completed an educational program were also more likely to successfully fulfill their future roles as mothers and citizens. It was felt that obtaining an education further bolstered a girl's personal virtue, which could help her overcome any desire to give in to evil tendencies. Subjects taught at the school included reading, spelling, writing, arithmetic, geography and grammar. Girls were divided into two groups, and group one would begin attending classes after breakfast, while group two tended to domestic training. Later in the day, the two groups would swap assignments so that each girl could participate in both endeavors each day.[90]

Domestic science class. *State Library of Iowa.*

To round out their daily exercises, the girls were also encouraged to engage in religious contemplation. In general, the young women were provided spaces and time to reflect in meditation or private prayer as opposed to being directly pressured or required to participate in religious services. Opportunities were available for girls to attend bible study groups and regular services, but Lewelling felt that they were more likely to come to the right conclusions on their own if they were provided opportunities to personally explore and reflect on their spirituality.[91]

The three-tiered approach kept the girls occupied, and most sources point to a well-ordered and congenial family-like atmosphere at the facility. However, given the nature of the facility, behavioral problems did arise. Perhaps unsurprisingly, considering Lorenzo Lewelling's approaches to other aspects of the school, he also took a more peaceful approach when it came to discipline. He felt that the girls were not evil and that they were only acting out on account of their environments. As a result, he did not think they deserved harsh punishments or reprimands but rather could benefit from a series of rewards or the loss of those rewards.

Lewelling implemented a system of marks and credits that guided the disciplinary structure in the Industrial School. Girls were able to accumulate marks and credits that could ultimately cut time off their sentences if they had finished their required training and studies. Marks could be earned for good behavior, and the marks were aggregated into the credits that counted toward release. The system of marks and credits likely helped bolster the school's ability to maintain a harmonious environment, but there were situations when the system was not enough to dissuade certain bad behaviors. In those cases, girls were to remain in bed in their rooms until they agreed to "do better."[92]

In the years spanning 1869 to 1900, 804 girls were sent to the reform school. Most were in their teens when they were sent to the facility, and many came from circumstances of extreme poverty, homes where one or both parents had died, jobs they were forced to work at early ages, urban settings and more. Approximately half of the girls incarcerated during that time were European immigrants and "American blacks." Many Black children coming to Iowa at the time were from families of newly freed slaves, and racism was prevalent, as were concerns about immigrant populations. Authorities focused their attentions more frequently on these populations, which resulted in higher than average rates of incarceration for these groups.[93]

During that same time, 93 percent of the girls in the industrial school were incarcerated for one of five reasons: incorrigibility, vagrancy, larceny, disorderly conduct and prostitution. Of that number, 64 percent were judged incorrigible, 11 percent vagrant and fewer than 8 percent represented the remaining categories. Similar trends were seen in adult women's prison populations, and their adult counterparts were also overwhelmingly incarcerated for crimes against public decency, as opposed to violent crimes against persons.[94]

While the statistics help paint the picture of trends and societal expectations at the time, some of the stories illustrate the truly dire situations that many of the state's youngest citizens encountered. Anna K. was a young German immigrant who found herself in the reform school after an unimaginably difficult road. Anna and her mother were living in Germany while her father was serving in the United States Cavalry. Anna and her mother began their journey to join her father, but during the journey, her father passed away, and Anna was separated from her mother. Anna, now on her own, was raped and became pregnant. It is unknown precisely how she survived, but after failing to secure any assistance going door-to-door soliciting help with barely any English speaking abilities, she somehow managed to make it through the winter. She delivered her own child, alone, in an outbuilding. She fell weak and ill and was ultimately unable to nurse her baby. It was speculated that under this stress she drowned her baby and was sent to the reform school for her crime. Superintendent Lewelling personally felt that it was the despair from her situation and her circumstances that led her to take the life of her child.[95]

Anna was not the only immigrant whose path to the school was chronicled. An Irish immigrant, Netty O., was incarcerated for stealing a loaf of bread from a bakery. Her parents had deserted her, and eventually, she resorted to theft for food. On being caught, she was sent to the reform school for burglary.[96]

Residents on wagon. *Douglas Wertsch, "Iowa's Daughter's: The First Thirty Years of the Girls Reform School of Iowa, 1869–1899,"* Annals of Iowa *49 (1987).*

The absence of Anna's and Netty's parents certainly played a role in their paths to incarceration, but there were also many girls at the school with parents who were present but simply could not afford them. Luella H., a young Black girl, was taken before a judge by her mother, who claimed she was incorrigible. In fact, Luella was not at all incorrigible, but her mother claimed that she was in an attempt to secure safe housing and sufficient food for her daughter. It was reported that at the trial Matron Lewelling was sympathetic and took Luella into the institution, even though she knew the mother's story was not true. It was noted in the docket that the matron accepted Luella in an effort to ease the family's burden.[97]

Another girl, Marilu G., was sent to the school after her mother died while the two were living in a poorhouse. After her mother's death, Marilu was too young to remain at the poorhouse alone, and she did not have any other family members to whom she could be sent. Unlike Luella and Marilu, some girls were confined in the reform school not because their parents were poor but because their parents were dangerous. Multiple girls were reported as incorrigible so their mothers could remove them from home situations where the girls were raped or abused by family members.[98]

Many of the young women fell into Lewelling's theory that those committing crimes were often victims of their environment. However, there were girls at the facility who were raised in wealthy homes and by loving parents. One such girl was sent to the reform school after attempting to poison her parents by putting rat poison in their coffee. Fortunately, her father was a physician, and he knew right away that they had been poisoned and was able to get help. This young individual became the only girl in the reform school who was incarcerated for the crime of attempted murder. The governor of Iowa eventually offered her a pardon if she would agree to live in a convent for three years, until she turned eighteen, but she refused to do so and instead opted to remain at the reform school until her twenty-first birthday.[99]

The individual stories the Lewellings often shared in reports and records certainly conveyed a strong correlation between environment and incarceration. Nevertheless, the reports also demonstrated that there were some girls who had good upbringings and turned toward a life of crime just the same. In the late 1880s, another voice emerged whose theories were increasingly being applied to societal issues. Charles Darwin and contemporaries, like Herbert Spencer, were advancing theories such as "survival of the fittest," which led to social Darwinists positing that an individual's biology, not their environment, shaped their destiny. Spencer believed that "nature would gradually eradicate poverty, evil, and criminal behavior among human beings if left to itself." Similar sentiments were argued by others in a counter chorus to environmentalism and its supporters' beliefs that people are inherently good and can be reformed. At least in the state of Iowa, as it relates to the Girls School, Lewelling had a much greater influence on the general assembly than proponents of hereditarianism. Despite periods of questioning and scrutiny, the legislature frequently applauded the work of Mr. and Mrs. Lewelling and continued to support the reform school.[100]

Sadly, in 1888, Mrs. Lewelling passed away shortly after Mr. Lewelling resigned from his position as superintendent the year before. After her death, Lorenzo Lewelling wrote of his wife, "Her soul was so full of tenderness and pity that she yielded up her sweet life in motherly devotion...to the unfortunate children of the state."[101] Even without the Lewellings' leadership, the school continued to grow and strove to provide a safe and productive home for juvenile girls in need.[102]

Following the resignation of Lorenzo Lewelling in 1887 and the death of his wife, the facility was overseen by Superintendent C.C. Cory, a former teacher at the school, who maintained leadership at the facility until his health declined in 1897.[103] Following Cory's departure, a rapid succession of superintendents came through the girls school. First was the former assistant superintendent at the boys school, A.H. Leonard,[104] and his wife in 1898. They were quickly followed by James Miller that same year. Miller also served a short tenure and led until the governance of the facility transitioned to F.P. Fitzgerald by 1900.[105] Throughout the turn of the century, the school continued to experience additional growing pains. Steam heat was introduced, which alleviated many inconveniences, but then segued into the want for electric light. The population continued to grow and breached more than one hundred[106] from time to time during the 1890s and two hundred in the early 1900s. The growing population demanded additional facilities, a larger boiler room, new water closets with toilets, additional water wells, food preparation technologies, hospital accommodations, more staff and more efficient laundry services.[107]

Beyond merely requiring additional family homes or cottages to accommodate the growing number of girls, the housing situation grew more complicated as the population continued to diversify. Girls charged with more devious and violent crimes began arriving at the facility. With a focus on family atmosphere and abhorrence for punitive measures, some felt it became increasingly difficult to control such populations while maintaining the safety of other girls.[108] Additionally, a need emerged to separate older girls from those who were much younger, so separate play areas and kitchens were identified to keep the two age groups apart.[109]

The level of difficulty in addressing the needs of the population and keeping all residents well cared for was considerable, and the superintendent of the girls school was about to face an additional challenge with a change in state law. The increase in incorrigible girls being sent to the facility was met with a modification to the law, which increased the age of majority, the time at which a girl would be released, from eighteen to twenty-one. As a result of this new rule, any girls nearing their eighteenth year could now be held by the facility for an additional three years. Not surprisingly, some of the girls were not pleased by the prospect of spending additional time at the school, and some believed that it was this change in policy that led to the riot of 1898. While some argued that the girls were acting out because of the threat of prolonged incarceration, others blamed the cause of the riot on the fact that the girls facility was managed by men, and allegations surfaced of lashings with large, hard rubber tubes. In an editorial submitted by the *Woman's Standard*, it was posited that not a single man has any place in an institution designed for women, and a newly created board of control abolished the use of corporal punishment.[110] The precise causes for the riot might be debated, but the uprising left a lasting impact on the facility.

The rapid succession from A.H. Leonard's appointment as superintendent to Miller's tenure was sparked by a change in oversight rules guiding the institution. In 1898, the legislature dissolved the school's board of trustees and replaced it with a statewide board of control. This move brought with it policy changes implemented by the board of control, which included salary cuts for many positions, and it was no longer acceptable for the matron to be the wife of the superintendent, as was the case with A.H. Leonard and his wife. The change in policy resulted in Leonard's wife losing her position, and Leonard himself opted to resign as superintendent. Leonard and his wife were not the only employees to resign when the new policies were implemented, and many other staff also left after learning that their salaries were to be cut. The heavy loss in employees resulted in staffing shortages and led to the quick appointment of James Miller, a former clerical employee at the home for elderly soldiers in Marshalltown, Iowa.[111]

Miller began his duties as superintendent on October 1, 1898. Leonard had been described as a fatherly figure, much like his predecessors, who encouraged the young residents to seek him out if they needed something. Contrarily, Miller refused to speak with the girls and directed that they should only work with his new and inexperienced subordinates. The situation at the school began to deteriorate rapidly, and by October 22, 1898, a riot was brewing.[112]

On October 22, two inmates escaped from Building No. 2, although they were quickly recaptured. On their return, the supervisor of that building decided to punish all fifty of the residents instead of only the two girls who had escaped. All of the girls were sent to bed without supper, and they began to plan their riot shortly thereafter. After 10:30 that evening, several of the girls left their beds and proceeded to go around the facility, rousing other girls to join their cause. More girls continued to join the group, and they began destroying property and arming themselves with whatever they could find, including sewing shears and table legs to use as clubs.[113]

Superintendent Miller rang the bells to indicate that the facility was in distress, and soon after, twenty to thirty quickly deputized townspeople showed up to try to control the riot. The girls lobbed numerous items at the citizens and threatened them with weapons, which ultimately resulted in the local men retreating and turning the situation over to the sheriff's office. During the chaos, some girls stole bicycles and fled the facility, and some retreated to a local teacher's yard to separate themselves from the riot, but nearly two hundred girls participated in the drinking, destruction and debauchery of the riot. Many reporters used terminology like "savage" to describe the girls and wrote how surprised they were to hear the vulgar and sexual things the young women were allegedly saying, as well as the actions they were taking at the facility. Some of the girls had even snuck away with some of the male townspeople who had arrived loaded with liquor and cigarettes to engage in inappropriate acts. Several men, including a police officer, were indicted for a number of crimes, including lewdness and rape.[114] The intensity of the situation also included an incident where several of the girls were able to corner Superintendent Miller. Unarmed, the girls opted to bite Miller in an attempt to injure him.[115]

Roughly two hours after the riot began in earnest, the sheriff and ten deputies arrived at the facility. Regaining control of the facility was a dangerous and lengthy process. According to reporters, it took two men roughly thirty minutes for each individual girl they captured and took into custody in the chapel. After the riot was under control, approximately seventy girls who were considered ringleaders were removed from Mitchellville and taken to Polk County Jail in Des Moines. Once relocated, further issues surfaced at the jail.[116]

Though removed from the premises at Mitchellville, the girls had never actually been arrested and were not scheduled to appear in court. There was no law under which they could be held at the jail, and even more concerning was their proximity to the men who were housed within talking distance of their cell. Reports claimed that girls were being encouraged to enter houses of prostitution by other women being held in jail and that others were engaging in deeply inappropriate conversations with some of the men. According to reports, the girls were in fairly positive spirits while at the jail. It was their thought that if they could not be returned to the school in Mitchellville, then they would need to be released to their parents, considering the jail had no legal standing to keep them. Polk County Jail remained the holding facility for some time, as a result of the girls' refusal to return to the school and many of the school staff members' refusals to have them return. The sheriff tried to send several girls back in small groups, a process that varied in success level by attempt. Many of the girls had fallen sick in jail and were willing to go back to better conditions found in the school's infirmary. Some of the girls who remained in Polk County Jail tried to petition for their release, but instead, they found themselves shipped back to the Industrial School with extra sheriff's guards in tow. Once the girls returned to the facility, they kept their promise and again began destroying property. The girls were quickly locked in secured facilities.[117] Despite the attempts at resistance, the sheriff was ultimately able to move the girls back to the school in Mitchellville by roughly a dozen at a time.[118]

When nineteen girls remained at Polk County Jail, they were visited by Susan Glaspell, who would later go on to write about the Hossack murder that would land Margaret Hossack in Anamosa in 1901. Glaspell spent weeks with the girls and tried to look at their incarcerations and confinements through their perspectives instead of casting them as the "savages" that many other reporters at the time were inclined to do. One particular exchange chronicled by Glaspell occurred when a baby was brought into the jail. According to reports, the girls grew incredibly excited and passed the baby around "carefully and caressingly, petting it just as anyone would." One girl commented that it was too bad that a baby had to be in the jail, to which Glaspell responded, "Well, don't you think it's too bad to have you girls in here too?" Glaspell, child welfare advocates and prominent lawyer and politician Leonard Brown all seemed to appreciate that these were in fact children and humans deserving of dignity and proper treatment. Glaspell mused, "Out of it all will there come something both practical and humanitarian which can shape lives almost predestined to misery?"[119]

Small improvements followed the riots, though in the all-too-common nature of women's corrections, substantial improvements remained to be seen. Laws were passed that allowed girls deemed dangerous to be transferred to the women's unit at Anamosa as long as they were over fourteen years old. Additionally, Matron Wilson and one family manager, who were alleged to have perpetrated much of the corporal punishment, were forced to leave their positions. Superintendent Miller did not resign as a result of the riot, but the event almost surely counted as a mark against his record. After refusing a governor's pardon of one girl at the facility and following what others saw as "anti-Catholic bigotry," he finally resigned from his job as superintendent in 1900.[120]

Between 1900 and 1909, the industrial school was overseen by F.P. Fitzgerald. He was credited with a number of improvements during his tenure, such as hiring more teachers, adding more cottages and organizing more activities. Fitzgerald brought with him an approach to managing the institution that focused on a family-style philosophy in housing, opportunities for entertainment and an increased emphasis on appropriate womanly behaviors.[121]

By 1905, four family cottages were on the premises, and each cottage housed fifty girls. If the staff to girl ratio had maintained the 1875 ratio, there might have been six or seven staff members present in each cottage; however, by 1905, each cottage had only one family manager or matron. Even though the population increase brought more dangerous and deviant girls to the facility, the doors still were not locked, and the girls were trusted to remain on the premises. To maintain the atmosphere of trust and reward as opposed to punishment, the institution requested that the legislature remove the more dangerous girls to better suited institutions throughout the state.[122]

In addition to an increase in the number of girls arriving at the facility, the school was also experiencing a literacy crisis. Almost 90 percent of the girls were considered illiterate on their arrival at the facility, but fortunately, a strong education department was available, and attendance was required. Into the twentieth century, the half-day industrial training and half-day educational training model was preserved. Half of the girls would go to school and half to domestic services from 7:15 to 11:30 a.m., and then they returned to their individual cottages for lunch. After lunch, those two halves of the population would switch either to education or domestic services, whichever they had not done in the morning, and that training would occur from 1:15 until 5:30 p.m. The girls would return for dinner in their cottages and engage in an additional study period.[123]

Cottage no. 2. *Mary Noble Collection, Iowa Women's Archives, University of Iowa Libraries, Iowa City.*

The domestic services offered by 1906 included dressmaking, laundry, cooking, dormitory maintenance and hospital work under the doctor's care. Training was also available in stenography and typewriting. The education department was divided into ten grades that a student could move through as they completed the material. Subjects offered included, but were not limited to, botany, algebra, history and reading. In addition to the training and educational opportunities, the girls were also allowed to participate in recreational activities, such as tennis, basketball and lawn games. Emphasis was also placed on music, and musical activities were available on a fairly regular basis.[124]

The availability of domestic and educational opportunities was critical for reform efforts; however, many girls chose to leave the school without completing training once they reached the age of majority. Additionally, due to overpopulation and a lack of space, some girls were pushed out before they were completely ready to reenter society. As a result, a request was put in for a state agent to be hired who could follow up with girls after they left the school on parole.[125] Within almost a year, a somewhat shockingly quick turnaround time in the field of female corrections, the first state agent for the facility, Ms. Clare Lunbeck, was hired. Results following the placement of individuals on parole indicated that girls paroled to work positions tended to fare much better than those who had been paroled into parental custody. It was also reported that girls paroled to work positions in country homes tended to do better than those paroled to work in city homes. In fact, during

Girls School Orchestra. *Douglas Wertsch, "Iowa's Daughter's: The First Thirty Years of the Girls Reform School of Iowa, 1869–1899,"* Annals of Iowa *49 (1987).*

one biennial period, almost all of the girls paroled to urban homes had been returned.[126] It is possible that the causes for the return of girls paroled to urban areas were twofold: many girls sent to work in urban areas might have been recruited to work in brothels, and other girls might have been more easily lured into other illegal or legal money-making opportunities that caused them to leave their paroled position.

In the period from 1909 to 1911, some girls might have lacked much incentive to stay at the industrial school and many likely dreaded returning to it for violating parole. In 1909, a new superintendent, Hattie Garrison, was appointed, and individuals perhaps hoped that a female superintendent would bring great improvements to the all-girls institution. Unfortunately, reports indicate that Garrison undid much of what Fitzgerald had developed. She considered many sports unladylike and banned girls from playing most of them. Allegations also surfaced that "Garrison had choked a young inmate and punched her in the face."[127] During Garrison's time at the institution, a second riot erupted, when twenty-five girls escaped and headed to Des Moines with the intention of discussing their treatment with the board of control. After their capture and return to the institution, violence once again broke out at the school.[128]

Girls at the facility were likely pleased that Garrison was replaced a short time later. On April 1, 1911, Mrs. Lucy M. Sickels was appointed as superintendent.

Like many of her predecessors, Sickels brought changes to the school. Doors were now locked with a key, which, based on the design of the structure, might have presented a fire hazard, and electric locks were suggested. The facility was in search of a dentist and eye doctor, and dormitories that existed in some of the cottages were being converted into rooms.[129]

The number of cottages had increased to six, but not all of the buildings were being used efficiently or fairly. Women were not equally subjugated and shortchanged in the correctional system; Black girls were often further mistreated. A separate cottage was requested to house the Black girls because White girls were not permitted to reside in the same cottages with them. As a result, a cottage built to house forty girls was shared by only eleven.[130]

Conditions at the school temporarily worsened when a well pump gave out, and the facility was without water from June to October in 1912. During that time, a barn was hit by lightning, and without water to fight the fire, the barn burned to the ground. Despite some of the setbacks that took place in the 1910s, the school was meeting with great success in reforming girls and finding them positions in the community. During this period, the majority of girls were successful while on parole, and relatively few were returned to the facility for parole violations.[131] However, that trend would begin a slow downward trajectory in the years to come.

Cottage no. 6. *Mary Noble Collection, Iowa Women's Archives, University of Iowa Libraries, Iowa City.*

A view of the Girls School campus. *Mary Noble Collection, Iowa Women's Archives, University of Iowa Libraries, Iowa City.*

Once again, the name of the facility was changed, and by the biennial report of 1918, the legislature adjusted the name from an industrial school to a training school. Domestic sciences slightly evolved as World War I raged on, and the girls worked to support the Red Cross through activities such as knitting various items.[132] In the 1920s, it became more difficult to find job placement opportunities. As a result, more girls were sent to work in urban areas, and parole violation rates began to rise. According to the state agent at the time, Ms. Ray M. Hanchett, the demand for girls to be placed in homes as domestic help had lowered. Despite the decrease in work positions, the training school officials worked hard to place parolees in jobs as opposed to back with their families.[133]

The hard work paid off, and within a couple years, demand for girls to take on domestic roles in rural areas was again on the rise. The number of girls who returned for parole violations once again dropped to an astoundingly low rate, and, in this case, settled below 1 percent. Former state agent Hanchett was promoted to superintendent,[134] a regular dentist was secured and more positive correspondence flowed in from graduates.[135]

More attention soon began to shift toward education, which was made apparent by regular requests for a school building and increased calls for educational opportunities for girls, now often referred to as "students," on parole. The emphasis on education was partially exemplified by the administration of a Stanford-Binet intelligence test in the late 1920s. The 1928 report submitted to the legislature shared the test results: "5% superior, 17% average, 13% dull normal, 19% borderline, 43% morons, and 3% imbeciles."[136] For a few years, the emphasis on education continued, and more paroled girls were allowed to attend school instead of being placed in jobs. However, it quickly became clear that the majority of girls paroled to pursue an education, 83 percent, returned in a relatively short amount of time. Of those who persisted through school for a longer amount of time, only one graduated.[137] Unfortunately, by the time the state agent returned her focus to placing parolees in rural positions, demand for domestic help had once again decreased.[138]

Education and parole continued as bedfellows into the 1930s as the training school developed various levels of parole classification and accompanying procedures based on the intelligence of the parolee. Students who tested at a normal or dull normal level of intelligence were classified into one group eligible for parole, and the state agents worked to place them in positions outside the institution. A second group was created that consisted of girls identified as having a borderline mental deficiency, and these students were still eligible for parole arrangements, assuming a circumstance with extra supervision could be provided. The third group consisted of students classified as "feebleminded." Instead of placing such girls on parole, the individuals were transferred to various institutions around the state, such as the Institution for Feebleminded Children and the Psychopathic Hospital.[139]

The focus on mental ability was not unique to the training school. In fact, the state established a Department of Psychology in 1934, and one of the department's functions was to assess juveniles held at various facilities around the state and make recommendations for any students who should be transferred to institutions better equipped to deal with various mental conditions.[140]

Around the same time that the state started allocating more resources to mental health, in tandem with an increase in attention to child welfare, Iowa also started practicing efficiency in the Board of Control of State Institutions. Since the nineteenth century, institutions around the state reported on the conditions of their facilities every two years, and many did so with great depth and detail. Unfortunately, the efficiency of the board of control came at a cost, and the detailed records of day-to-day activities and operations at institutions, such as the Training School for Girls, instead gave way to statistical spreadsheets and policy language on admissions protocol.

Despite thorough reports from superintendents becoming scarcer, Superintendent Anny Lynam contributed a report to the board of control that exemplified that the conditions of the early 1940s appeared to mostly continue on in the tradition of the decades prior. Education and vocational training continued to be valued, various extracurricular activities were provided and the institution was frequently in need of updated facilities. By 1940, girls could only be admitted to the training school if they were between the ages of ten and eighteen, although several girls remained until twenty. Most girls entering the facility were classified as delinquent, incorrigible or both. The number of girls sent to the school for offenses such as prostitution was smaller than in previous decades.[141]

In addition to the decrease in girls being admitted to the training school for crimes such as prostitution, there was also an overall reduction in commitments, a fact mentioned by Superintendent Lynam and her successor, Superintendent Marie L. Carter, in 1946. After a brief surge in the population between 1943 and 1944, the numbers again decreased.[142] Carter mentioned that many more of the girls being committed might be better suited to state psychiatric or feebleminded institutions, and she also boasted that the state's child welfare effort played a vital role in helping with the success of parolees returning to their homes or communities. While the girls remaining in the school enjoyed extra space and more one-on-one attention as the population declined, they were still in want for a gymnasium to provide recreation in the winter months and desperate for trained personnel in the school programs and department director positions.[143]

By the time the 1950s arrived, Superintendent Carter reported that the population had held fairly consistent around one hundred girls. This lower number provided an opportunity for staff to work with girls more thoroughly, which was especially important considering that new commitments continued to arrive with lower-than-average intelligence quotients. The training school was also in the second year of a cosmetology program that was meeting with great success, and a new school and administration building had been completed. The new building provided the long-awaited gymnasium, in addition to classrooms, a library, a stage and a music room, and would continue to support these uses even after incarcerated adults later moved to the facility. The state agents at the time, Dora Barz and Lenna T. Boots, also reported that parolees were doing well. Once again, fewer girls were returned to their homes on parole and were instead situated in employment opportunities. Although the wild success in the rehabilitation of girls during the time of the Lewellings might have been a thing of the past, the state agents and superintendent of the 1950s were working hard to improve the odds of success for juvenile girls coming through the training school.[144] In addition to the construction of the administration building in 1950, nearly all of the original structures had been replaced by new housing units built primarily in the 1960s, with the exception of one that had been built in 1933.[145]

Despite the reports of dedicated staff, new programs and buildings and a commitment to the success of parolees, the tenure of Superintendent Carter was not always cast in a positive light. A number of former residents and late Iowa senator Minnette Doderer brought forth concerns of mistreatment at the school. In 1972, a report to the state listed a number of complaints.

The legislative investigation concluded that too frequently girls were placed in solitary confinement for an average of nine days and even twenty-two days at the most extreme. House mothers were accused of publicly posting the residents' menstrual cycles, girls were only allowed to write letters twice a week and physicals were allegedly performed by individuals who were not registered doctors or nurses and in a purportedly degrading manner. Additionally, silence rules were implemented that disallowed girls to speak except when passing between classes and at meals, and girls were still locked in rooms with no way to get out or call for someone in the event of an emergency. Concerns existed about the quality of education, which fell below the state's legal requirement.[146] After the concerns surfaced and many staff members resigned, reports indicated the situation improved at the facility.

A short time later, the training school came under fire from members of the legislature who believed it duplicated services offered at the Iowa Juvenile Home in Toledo, Iowa. As of 1976, only fifty-four girls remained in the facility, and such a number could be transferred to the other juvenile institution. In truth, many others disagreed because the training school offered "individualized treatment and educational opportunities" that were not necessarily paralleled at the facility in Toledo.[147] The legislative calls to close the facility continued into 1977, when the legislature handed down an appropriations budget that was $47 million below what the State Department of Social Services needed to operate facilities throughout the state.[148] Despite the calls to close the facility, it managed to continue functioning as a training school for girls until adult women were transferred to the premises in 1982. The remaining girls were transferred to Toledo, the last remaining juvenile facility for Iowan girls, which would close permanently at the order of Governor Branstad in 2014 after reports of abuse. After the closure, female juveniles were transferred out of state.[149]

4

WOMEN'S REFORMATORY AT ROCKWELL CITY

I n May 1918, many decades before incarcerated women would ever step foot in the current Mitchellville facility, twenty-two women were transferred from Anamosa's penitentiary to the new and first women-only facility in Rockwell City, Iowa. While in Anamosa, the women had been secluded inside a solitary building known as the Female Department, and what they found at the Women's Reformatory in Rockwell City was perhaps a more welcome sight. With no men present, the women would have more access to the facility, which, when it opened on June 1, 1918, included an administration building, one completed cottage for housing the women, a power house, an industrial building, a schoolhouse and a second housing cottage that was almost complete. The property also included over two hundred acres, twenty-five of which were set aside for gardening, while much of the rest was intended for farming.[150]

Compared to the earlier facilities where women had been held, the new Rockwell City site was a significant improvement; however, it cannot be overlooked how long it took for women to finally inhabit a state-funded institution designed and built for them alone. It was not until almost eighty years after Iowa's first prison opened, double the amount of time it took men to get a second facility, that women in the state were finally housed in an institution that was designed to better meet their specific needs. By the close of the first year at Rockwell City, twenty-five women had been committed to the institution. The average sentence was one to five years, and women were still largely being committed for crimes against society, such as lewdness and transmission of disease.[151]

Administration Building at the Women's Reformatory at Rockwell City in 1920. *Mary Noble Collection, Iowa Women's Archives, University of Iowa Libraries, Iowa City.*

Lena Beach, the first superintendent of the institution, noted in her first biennial report that a pathology building was being constructed for holding new arrivals for assessment. The structure would not be completed for a few more years, but it showed attention to the idea of classification and ensuring women were housed and treated in the most appropriate way possible for the individual. Beach also noted that many women were deficient in domestics, so experience in sewing, gardening and cooking was offered at the new reformatory.[152]

By 1920, two years after the reformatory opened, 104 women had been through the facility. At the end of that period, 51 were in confinement, 84 percent were White, 16 percent were Black and the majority were between the ages of fifteen and twenty-five years old. Four times as many women were incarcerated for crimes against society than for any other offense. During that same period of time, state agent Genevieve Henderson was available to help secure opportunities for women on parole. To better ensure a successful transition back into society, classes in writing, spelling and shorthand had also been implemented. While training in education and domestics was critical, so was maintaining a healthy mind, so small entertainments and a library were also available to the women.[153]

The incarcerated women enjoyed a relative amount of freedom, especially by modern definitions, in the Rockwell City reformatory. The facility had no fences or gates, and the institution had an open-door honor system. Despite the lack of locks and fences, there were few attempts to escape, and there were 112 women in confinement by the end of the 1922 period, which doubled the number from two years before. Furthermore, only one inmate was returned from parole during that period, and there were no recommitments.[154] During the same period, Lena Beach resigned as superintendent to take a similar position in Minnesota, and Eleanor Hutchinson took her place.[155]

Near the end of Hutchinson's first couple of years as superintendent, the institution seemed to be in full swing. The pathology cottage had been completed, a slaughterhouse was built, an old granary was rebuilt and a cattle shed was erected. To solve earlier water shortages, a well was sunk deeper, providing more water, and fruit trees, chickens and milk from the cows provided plenty of sustenance. The animals and farming also provided opportunities for women to learn valuable skills and stay active. Even though there was plenty to do to keep the institution running smoothly, Hutchinson called for more opportunities for the women to engage in additional occupations. She wanted them to have employment that could make both the women and the institution money and to further enhance the sustainability of the reformatory.[156]

Despite the advances in agricultural, domestic and entertainment opportunities, not all was well at the reformatory. By the end of 1924, the population was at 111 women, and the institution was crowded. When the

A partial view of the grounds at the Women's Reformatory. *Mary Noble Collection, Iowa Women's Archives, University of Iowa Libraries, Iowa City.*

reformatory was initially built, the plan was for each woman to have her own room, but the growth in the population soon required two to a room. During that time, prison officials were quoted as saying that it was "undesirable" to house "colored girls" with White girls, which added an additional challenge to the rooming ratios. Another area in which overcrowding occurred was in the employee rooms. Female employees lived on site, and they were experiencing similar overcrowding as the prisoners. Employees were forced to stay two to a room, and the superintendent was taking up the space above the office for lack of anywhere else to live. Hutchinson requested a separate superintendent cottage be erected so the employees could stay in the space above the office she was inhabiting.[157]

As the reformatory headed into its sixth year and the 1920s rushed forward, the demographics and crimes began to shift. In years prior, most women were committed for crimes against society, but more were starting to come to the reformatory for crimes against the government, such as violating the Harrison Drug Act and the National Prohibition Act. Additionally, many women were arriving with diseases, such as syphilis and gonorrhea. The reformatory also started to experience more escapes and women returning to the institution while on parole. As of 1924, the rate of successfully releasing women into society or having them complete parole had dropped from 93 percent to 85 percent.[158]

Despite the increased number of escape attempts, the facility still remained unfenced, and the number of escapes climbed once again, totaling eighteen attempts in the period of 1924 to 1926. While no fences had been built, cells were available for solitary confinement, and twenty-two women were sent to those cells in the two-year period. Some of the increased issues with behavior might have been due to changes in sentencing terms. Many of the women were being sent for short three- to-six-month commitments, and officials complained that there was not enough time to reform these women, so they merely became disruptions to the institution. In addition to an increase in women being sent to the facility with shorter sentences, women with longer than average incarceration times were added to the population as well. The average incarceration time of one to five years increased by 1926, and over half the women had sentences of five to ten years, and fourteen women had ten- to-fifteen-year sentences.[159]

During the mid-1920s, physical additions to the facility included the beginnings of a perimeter fence and a wrought-iron gate that was added to the entrance. The last piano was purchased so that each cottage had one, and by 1926, cottage no. 2 was being used exclusively to treat venereal disease patients and as a receiving ward. Although a number of women were treated for diseases, only one death occurred between 1924 and 1926, and the victim was a seven-week-old baby who had been born to one of the women and suffered from spina bifida. The diseases and escapes certainly presented some problems for the institution, but officials still reported that the overall situation and behavior at the reformatory was excellent.[160]

In 1927, Superintendent Hutchinson resigned to take a position at a federal women's institution, and Pauline E. Johnston took over, until her death in 1945.[161] Toward the beginning of Johnston's tenure as superintendent, the population stayed around one hundred women, but the capacity of the facility and its now three cottages was only seventy-eight. Johnston requested a fourth cottage from the board of control and continued to ask for the auditorium and gymnasium requested by her predecessor.

By 1931, the auditorium was completed with space in the basement to be used for recreation, and a flag industry had been added so the women could make American flags for the schools and state institutions around Iowa. Although some improvements were being made, the calls for another cottage or hospital continued unanswered, which led to the mixing of better-behaved women with ones who were more dangerous.[162]

Even into the 1930s, the reformatory still had no armed guards or fence around it, although it did have "ornamental bars" on the windows, and women were locked in their rooms at night. In keeping with the softer touch of no fences and few bars, the women also seemed to view Superintendent Johnston as more of a mother figure, and they affectionately referred to the institution as the little city of Lanedale, a name that stuck throughout the remaining days of the facility. Johnston referred to the women as "youngsters," and she seemed willing to involve them in decisions, such as planning a spontaneous baseball game or what uniform to wear when farming the now five hundred acres of land. Women who had babies at the reformatory were allowed to keep their infants with them for nine months, and women were also allowed to add personal touches to their daily dress, such as handkerchiefs they made themselves. While reformatory life included many activities, such as the symphony and dressmaking, order was still kept and rules were enforced, like eating breakfast and lunch in silence, rising at 5:00 a.m. to begin work and observing lights out at 9:00 p.m.[163]

In 1947, Helen M. Talboy was hired as the new superintendent at the reformatory. Talboy had been a registered nurse in World War II and served in nations including Italy and Africa. In many of the 1940s newspaper articles written about Talboy, reporters felt the need to refer to her as the "attractive

COTTAGE NO. 3 WOMENS REFORMATORY, ROCKWELL CITY, IA.

A picture of cottage no. 3 taken between 1920 and 1940. *Mary Noble Collection, Iowa Women's Archives, University of Iowa Libraries, Iowa City.*

superintendent." Under the supervision of the "attractive" Helen Talboy, daily life remained much the same at the reformatory, which was still referred to as Lanedale by "girls," or inmates, in residence. Women were still allowed to decorate their rooms, put on plays for the public and add personal touches to their blue uniforms. The women were now allowed to speak to each other during lunch, although breakfast was still taken in silence. One of the few but significant changes enacted while Talboy remained superintendent was that by the late 1940s, babies were no longer allowed to stay in the facility after the women gave birth. Talboy and some of the prisoners believed that it was too hard on the women and other residents when the babies were allowed to stay so long on the premises. As a result, after the baby was born off-site, he or she would be immediately taken from the mother and placed with the family or state agency.[164]

Some might have found it hard to understand the shift in relocating the babies born to the women when Talboy herself adopted a baby in 1950 and brought him to live with her on the premises. According to Talboy, the women in the facility were happy to have the baby around, and Talboy was showered with gifts for the baby from members of the board of control and board of parole. Diapers and baby clothes could been seen hanging from the clothes lines at the facility, serving as a constant reminder of the child on the grounds. As Talboy reported, this might have been a happy sight for many of the women at the facility, but it was no doubt challenging for others to see a mother and child engaging with one another when the women themselves might have been separated from children of their own.[165]

Alongside the few changes made to daily life around the institution were shifts in the reasons for incarceration. During World War II, incarceration rates dropped nationally,[166] and the war might have contributed to the reformatory housing roughly half its standard population of around one hundred when Talboy arrived. Talboy posited that the war had an impact on incarceration rates afterward, as well. She suggested that individuals who were able to find work in the plants during the war became accustomed to a level of income that was not sustainable once the troops returned home. Now used to life in a higher income bracket, some women resorted to forgery, which landed them in prison. When Talboy took over the institution, the population averaged thirty-five to forty-eight inmates, but after the war ended, the population increased to seventy-two women.[167] Superintendent Talboy also believed that barbiturates, liquor and other drugs played a significant role in the downfall of many women, and she reported that over half of the committed women admitted to the use of alcohol.[168]

In 1953, Helen Talboy left the institution, and Mrs. Elda Kyles became the superintendent.[169] The years under Kyles's influence seemed to mirror the time of her predecessors. The reformatory continued to provide an environment that was more personal and allowed for many of the comforts of home when contrasted to modern correctional institutions. Even in Kyles's reporting to the board of control, she personally notes her goal that the cottages feel as much like home to the women as possible. The women were allowed to decorate their private rooms, which included an in-room lavatory and stool. Each floor of the cottages had a tub and shower, and women were allowed a number of entertainments in the cottages, including a television, radios, a piano and a phonograph. These entertainments were purchased through the Women's Entertainment Fund, which was financed by the women.[170]

Women were also allowed to use cosmetics as long as they did not misuse them, and they were allowed to bring in some of their own clothing, such as slippers and housecoats. They were also provided with health, dental and psychological support. At times during Kyles's tenure, physician availability varied from full time to visiting twice a week with on-call availability. A dentist and an oculist were available on contract, and three part-time psychologists were at the reformatory three times a week. On entry to the institution, women were held in isolation to undergo a period of medical exams and mental tests by the Classification Committee. If a woman was found to have a need for substantial mental care, she would be transferred to the Mental Health Institute in Cherokee, Iowa. Otherwise, women would enter various educational and training programs offered by the institution. The Classification Committee served as a vehicle for determining the best education and training routes for each woman based on her needs and history, as well as her physical and mental situation.[171]

In addition to the formal education and training programs offered at the reformatory, Kyles believed that it was important to provide structure for leisure time. According to Kyles, it was "necessary that interest should be developed for the leisure hours, not only in the institution, but when an inmate returns to society." Recreation offerings included arts and crafts, as well as opportunities to exert physical energy. The reformatory hosted games of softball, volleyball and ping-pong, and it also coordinated dances, plays, parties and movie showings. For women interested in religion, opportunities existed for them to attend services or classes, although religious engagement was not compulsory.[172]

While structure was provided for the personal growth and engagement of the women, there were activities that benefitted the institution and state, as well. Women were allowed to work in the sewing industry and manufactured inmate apparel, sleeping garments, hospital gowns, tea towels, napkins, tablecloths and draperies. They also assisted with gardening and farming the over two hundred acres set aside for various agricultural activities, including the care of cattle, swine and poultry.[173]

The education, training, work and recreational opportunities gave the women a sense of purpose and likely made time at the reformatory a bit easier or more comfortable. The private rooms provided to women also certainly contributed to the homelike feel of the institution, and during times when the reformatory was forced to house women two to a room, officials were displeased. What might have contributed to the need to house two women in one room during this time period was the fact that, unlike men, women were not allowed to be held in jails for sentences longer than thirty days.[174] Superintendents Talboy and Kyles both expressed concerns with jail sentences being served at Rockwell City, while county jails could provide housing for male prisoners beyond thirty days. Kyles worried that the influx of short term women created large turnover, and it likely caused regular interruptions to the culture of reform and improvement.[175]

The image of the Women's Reformatory can evoke a sense of pastoral calmness mixed with cordiality and respect for one another. While portions

Women sewing in the reformatory. *State Historical Society of Iowa, Iowa City.*

of that image might have been true at many times, it was still an institution meant to confine those who had committed an offense, and as such, problems were bound to arise. The institution preferred to focus on prevention of potential issues and took a three-tiered approach to try to mitigate the need for disciplinary action. The leadership of the facility believed in and promoted good guidance and counseling, an honor time system and the Inmate Council.[176]

Instead of having any individual offenses dealt with exclusively by the superintendent or another employee, a guidance committee existed that would consider any issues as a group. Additionally, the women were also allowed to elect one representative from their own cottage to represent their interests in any cases that might be brought forward. The Inmate Council could work with the employee guidance committee on individual cases but also when addressing large issues or general welfare in the institution. In addition to the two groups, the reformatory also had an honor time system, which allowed ten extra days to be removed from a sentence for every thirty days served without incident. In Kyles's report to the board of control in 1962, she noted that in many cases women were able to shorten sentences of years by months.[177]

Kyles and her staff might have had a somewhat easier time preventing behavioral incidents than their counterparts at men's facilities due to the nature of crimes committed by the women in the reformatory. The vast majority of the women incarcerated were serving time for nonviolent crimes, as well as crimes that could not likely be repeated in a prison setting. In 1962, 80 percent of the women at Rockwell City were being held for forgery and 13 percent for sex or moral crimes. During the same time, only one woman was incarcerated for murder in the second degree, and two were serving sentences for manslaughter. While women were still predominantly being committed for nonviolent crimes, those numbers would begin to fluctuate in the decades to come.[178]

A change for the institution took place in the late 1960s, when the women found themselves under the leadership and supervision of the first male superintendent. The information available during this time in the reformatory's history is limited, and it appears that sometime around 1966 James E. Allen was appointed as the acting superintendent of the women's reformatory. Allen had been at the Boys Training School in Eldora prior to

Superintendent Elda M. Kyles behind her desk, presumably with other reformatory staff. *State Historical Society of Iowa, Iowa City.*

arriving in Rockwell City. Around the same time, the Iowa Board of Control sought a law change through the 1967 legislature, requesting that it overturn the law stating that the head of the Women's Reformatory at Rockwell City needed to be female.[179]

According to the limited available sources, the reformatory might have begun to approach new financial challenges in 1967. It is challenging to determine the source of the difficulties and whether or not they began prior to Allen's arrival. Furthermore, it is important to note that the reformatory continued to face financial challenges following Allen's departure. A newspaper article written in 1967 indicated that expenses at the reformatory had increased by 27.3 percent, although the number incarcerated had decreased from seventy-eight to sixty women. During the same period, the staff increased from forty to forty-five employees.

The previous expenses had been $227,451 for the reformatory, and in 1967, the expenses rose to $353,226. The article stated that no specific reasons had been provided for the change in cost, but that an auditor "criticized some account procedures" and claimed that a "cigar box" style of accounting was being used at the institution. The auditor made additional accounting recommendations, such as pre-numbering receipts and depositing them weekly. Other cost increases outlined included a 24.4 percent increase in administrative costs, a 59.6 percent cost increase in care and treatment, an 18.0 percent housing increase and a 3.8 percent bump in plant operations. Decreases included institutional revenues dropping nearly 13.5 percent and farm and garden earnings decreasing by 56.5 percent.[180]

Information was more limited during this brief time, other than that it appears Allen left the institution shortly after his appointment as acting superintendent. It was reported that Allen met his future wife while the two worked together at the reformatory, and the pair married in 1967. Sometime after their marriage, the couple moved to Indianola, Iowa, and Laurel Rans became the new superintendent of the institution.[181]

Rans's arrival at the Women's Reformatory resulted in a circling back to a phenomenon perhaps more common in female institutions. As with former superintendent Talboy, newspaper writers once again began focusing on Rans's looks almost as much as the institution itself. On meeting Rans at the airport, reporter Helen Weiershauser, commented, "I couldn't believe my eyes! She didn't resemble any prison matron I had seen on the TV movies. Before me stood an attractive looking young woman."[182] Perhaps Weiershauser's comment was providing a glimpse into many people's perspectives of what women's prisons should be in contrast to what they actually were. This image calls on a common societal misuse of prison as a means of separating feared members of society from the general population, as opposed to working to improve the individual and therefore the community as a whole. What some members of society likely realized, and certainly Rans did as well, was that the institution needed to be focused on treatment and not merely custody.[183]

Rans believed in rehabilitation and continued Kyles's previous efforts to provide training and a sense of self for the women. One of her changes was to allow women to wear clothing of their choice as opposed to the prison-issued uniforms they had been provided in the past. Rans felt that this change could help restore a sense of dignity to the women, and if the women could not afford their own clothing then items would be provided by the institution.[184] This restoration of dignity further exemplified Rans's commitment to rehabilitation and seeing the women for the people that they were. In another interview with Weiershauser, Rans was asked about staff safety. Rans reported, "We need no protection.…If a girl ever attacked any employe [sic] she would have all the other girls on her immediately. This is the kind of place this is. We care about each other."[185]

The way the press painted Talboy and Rans as "attractive" superintendents and the women's shared belief in the importance of opportunities for growth and training for the women were not their only similarities. Rans also favored less negatively loaded terminology with regard to the titles given to incarcerated women. Talboy had referred to the women as "girls" instead of inmates, and Rans preferred to refer to them as "clients."[186] With Rans's arrival at the reformatory, the opportunities for the women seemed to be set on a positive trajectory.

The situation improved even further for the clients when the legislature supported the creation of a work release program. It was felt that women might better reenter society with more assistance. The work release program allowed women to obtain positions and begin earning money before leaving the facility. Women participating in the work release program received full wages that were paid to the facility to cover institutional expenses such as food, lodging and clothing. Additional income could be used to pay off any financial obligations that the women might have incurred, such as child support.[187]

The work release program celebrated another significant gain when a halfway house opened in June 1969. While the work release program itself was a significant step forward for the women, the facility in Rockwell City, Iowa, was located hours away from the state's capital, Des Moines. As the

Women's Reformatory at Rockwell City was the only prison for women at the time, many of its inhabitants were not from the area, so participating in work release only in Rockwell City would not necessarily help them when they were ready to reenter society. The opening of the halfway house at 604½ School Street in the heart of Des Moines offered the women an opportunity to participate in the work release program in the city.[188]

The halfway house in Des Moines was initiated and supported by an individual donor and a local agency helping those in need, Bethel Mission. Josephine J. Thompson was a former registered nurse, and she stated in her will that her money should be used to help women in need after her death. Bethel Mission then approached Mrs. Phyllis Kocur, who was the parole and probation supervisor for the Bureau of Corrections Services at the time. With the goal of supporting the work that Superintendent Rans was currently doing at the facility in Rockwell City, Bethel Mission opened and remodeled some floors above its facility for the use of the halfway house.[189]

The timing of the work release program and garnishment of the women's wages likely alleviated a slight bit of the financial burden for the facility at Rockwell City, which was still facing many of the same monetary problems it encountered in the years before. As the facility transitioned from acting superintendent James E. Allen to Superintendent Laurel Rans, costs at the facility continued to rise, even when populations began to decrease. Governing bodies were starting to receive budget proposals, and the Women's Reformatory was a topic of conversation.

By 1969, the annual operating cost had risen almost another $50,000 a year to a total of $400,100.[190] Rans pointed to the cost per woman rising steadily over the years, noting that costs were high despite the population dropping from seventy-two clients to fifty over the two preceding years.[191] The increased use of parole and probation was identified as one of the causes for the declining population, yet Rans argued that the way the cost per woman was calculated continued to drive the total operating budget up. In a small attempt to reduce expenses, Rans cut the staff number back down after former Superintendent Allen had increased it two years before. She felt that fifty staff positions were too many, and she dropped that number back down to forty-four.[192]

The staff she retained included ten matrons for each cottage of twenty-eight to thirty women in the facility. In addition to the matrons' salaries, Superintendent Rans made a salary of approximately $11,000. Rans's decision to let women bring in their own clothes mitigated costs slightly, but the costs of housing the women and running the facility continued to increase.[193]

According to an article in the *Fort Dodge Messenger* in 1969, the Department of Social Services began putting forth budget proposals, which included addressing the costs of the Women's Reformatory. One proposal submitted to the House Appropriations Committee included the idea of closing the facility at Rockwell City and transferring the women to two state-run mental health facilities. This proposal threatened to return women to the time in Anamosa, when they were relegated to sharing a housing facility with the mentally ill men. Fortunately, Representative Joan Lipsky and a subcommittee felt that a more serious study needed to be conducted before any changes to the housing plan for Iowa's female prison population were made. Lipsky noted that Superintendent Rans had been running the facility very well and that it should continue operating at that time.[194]

Despite the murmur of pressures from the legislature, daily life at the reformatory continued on much as usual, with women continuing to engage in the community and taking advantage of educational and training opportunities. Though the overall environment sustained its somewhat peaceful existence, the women coming into the facility continued to change. By the 1970s, the system began to experience an increase in female incarcerations for crimes more typically associated with men.

Before the 1970s, Superintendent Rans estimated that two-thirds of the incarcerated women were serving sentences for crimes such as forgery and writing bad checks. In her report to the *Des Moines Register* in the fall of 1970, more than half of the women at Rockwell City were sentenced for crimes such as murder, manslaughter, assault with intent to commit injury, breaking and entering and other similar crimes. It is important to note, however, that these types of crimes typically carry longer sentences, so naturally, an institution will have a greater population of these individuals due to sentence length. Phyllis Kocur, director of the Women's Division at the Iowa Bureau of Adult Corrections, added that she was "sure it's a part of a kind of general emancipation of women....Almost never did we hear of women in such crimes as car theft or filling station holdups. Now this is pretty usual." Kocur went on to explain that while women sometimes initiated these more male-dominated crimes, they were often with men at the time who were also committing the illegal act. The scenario was not unique to Iowa, however, and Rans explained that the same trend could be seen nationwide.[195]

Rans went on to postulate that there were also important trends to note regarding the socioeconomic status of the women committing these new crimes against persons and property. Rans shared that women who were more assertive and lived at a lower socioeconomic level might not have had as many legal means to use their confidence to gain a leg up, such as through education or climbing a corporate ladder. Instead, they might have had to turn to illegal ways to attempt to improve their lot. In the same *Des Moines Register* article, Rans is quoted as saying, "We pretty well acknowledge that the people we see here at Rockwell City are—there's no other way to put it—POOR."[196]

Socioeconomics were not the only factor affecting the population at Rockwell City and other facilities across the country. While concerns regarding racial and age disparities were certainly raised to some extent in the past, new attention was being placed on these populations during this time period. Women at the reformatory partnered with community churches to present a conference for the public, prison leaders and members of the clergy to provide learning opportunities about other races and their experiences in the community. Videos, presentations and movies were used to help spur discussion about the topic.[197] Furthermore, Nolah H. Ellandson, the director of the Bureau of Adult Corrections, shared that there was also a strong correlation between crime and the trends of youth. Ellandson shared that 75 percent of crimes were committed by individuals who were under twenty-five years of age.[198]

Attention continued to stay on the reformatory and its women when the leadership transitioned from Laurel Rans to Ted Wallman in 1972. Wallman had been the assistant superintendent since 1970 under Rans and took over as acting superintendent after her resignation.[199] Shortly into Wallman's tenure, he began facing increasingly frequent calls to close the facility.

In May 1973, the Senate Appropriations Committee requested that a study be completed to determine if there were alternatives to closing the women's facility in Rockwell. One of the reasons for the proposal was to address the viability of the reformatory due to a declining population. The other argument made by the Senate was related to the availability of work release programs. Many facilities for men were opened nearer prisoners' hometowns, which allowed them to participate in more work release opportunities. The Senate lamented that such opportunities did not exist for most women, and they were simply all shipped away to the facility in Rockwell City, Iowa.[200]

In the other chamber, House representative R.G. "Hap" Miller, a representative for Rockwell City, did not agree with much of the Senate's assessment. While he did support the notion that women should have more options closer to their hometowns, he disagreed with the proposal of closing the facility. He thought that the costs of the facility were actually reasonable when compared to the costs of other state facilities for women.[201] Not only were the costs comparable to those of other women's facilities, but they were also comparable to some of the men's facilities in Iowa. In the period of 1974 to 1975, the yearly cost to house a man in the State Penitentiary at Fort Madison was $8,014, while the cost of housing a woman in Rockwell City was $8,089. One disparity was found when measuring against the cost at the men's reformatory in Anamosa, where the rate was $5,664 per inmate.[202]

While many people were in support of the facility at Rockwell City remaining open, all seemed to agree that there were a number of issues that still needed to be addressed, even if the reformatory were to remain in operation. By the 1970s, there were few work release programs and private or religious halfway houses available to women, in comparison to the facilities available to men. The opportunities for women to partake in such programs near their own communities were even more limited. State and prison officials wanted more community-based corrections opportunities, but the funding to expand those operations was not appropriated to make those goals a reality. Many women feared how they would integrate back into society after being released from the reformatory, and they were worried about how they could gain sufficient employment and housing without ultimately needing to use illegal means. The thoughts and concerns shared by the women were echoed by Superintendent Wallman. According to Wallman, "There are four types of institutions for men, plus a good halfway house system.…Yet facilities for women are few and far between."[203]

Wallman speculated that perhaps the disparity in the number of facilities between women and men was spurred by the greater amount of fear and fascination that society held for male criminals, as opposed to their female counterparts. It is possible that society at large still had a greater fear of male criminals, but as superintendents had reported and national trends had indicated, the typically "male-associated" crimes were beginning to be reflected more in the female population.[204]

Although the state did not provide funding for women's transition facilities, the American Association of University Women (AAUW) did receive a $1,000 grant in the spring of 1974 designed to aid women preparing to reenter their communities. The AAUW had recently conducted a study on the availability of women's opportunities post-release, and they arrived at the same conclusion as many prison and state officials. The state was not providing adequate reentry opportunities for women. After reaching this conclusion, the AAUW used its grant to begin to address the need for better transitional programming for women. The grant was not enough to be used on a facility, but it might have been a factor in the legislature's July 1973 change of law that stated women were allowed to leave the Rockwell City reformatory to engage in employment in their home community, provided they were under "supervised living conditions." The programming offered by the AAUW also included services focused on women finding jobs, locating housing and working on relationships. The grant afforded some promising situations for more women; however, many of them remained unable to take advantage of the AAUW's program. Although women had the chance to find a work situation in their home communities, they were often unable to secure a suitable location to satisfy the supervision component of their release.[205]

A couple years after the small gain of the AAUW grant, the reformatory continued to be bombarded by calls to vacate the facility. In February 1976, Representative Thomas Higgins of Davenport suggested that the women should be moved to a vacant building on the premises of the mental health institution at Mount Pleasant so that Rockwell City could be used for men who were facing overcrowding in Anamosa. Once again, women's interests appeared positioned to take a back seat for the needs of male inmates. To further what to many likely came across as an insult, the plan also suggested that the juvenile girls held at the State Training School in Mitchellville should be moved to the juvenile facility in Toledo so that male inmates who were close to the end of their sentence could be relocated to the Mitchellville facility. In sum, the proposal was to eliminate all facilities designed for women in an effort to further increase the far more numerous locations already in existence for men. As one might expect, the plan was considered inappropriate. Representative Joan Lipsky, who had advocated for the women seven years earlier, when the plan to move them to the state's mental health facilities was previously proposed, once again took issue with such a proposal. According to an article in the *Tribune*, Lipsky deemed the plan sexist and was outraged. Lipsky stated, "You'd put the women any damn place you want, and then worry about the men. You can't believe the women of Iowa will stand still for that kind of a program."[206] The record of the *Fort Dodge Messenger* reflected further sentiments from Lipsky, as well as other politicians and prison officials. Lipsky's additional comments reflected the deeply rooted state tradition of awarding primary correctional consideration to men, consistently at a cost to women. She made further statements, including, "I take great offense to the Higgins plan. It's main concern is finding a place to house male inmates, and doesn't show any compassion for the women at all….I wouldn't oppose a change if a better alternative were proposed, but to suggest just sticking the women any old place in order to solve the men's problem certainly is wrong....I shouldn't really be surprised though. That's the role women usually find themselves in."

Lipsky was certainly not alone in her criticisms of Higgins's proposal, and she was joined by politicians on both sides of the aisle. The House speaker, Dale Cochran, added that the issue was that the correctional system itself did not have enough space, and simply moving people from one place to another did not solve the broader issue of an overall statewide lack of space. Even the governor, Robert Ray, added that something needed to be done, but that the women's system could not be shifted into a situation where they would have less than they currently did.

Predictably, Superintendent Wallman also opposed the plan proposed by Higgins. Like many others, he was open to discussing suggestions, but he wanted to hear ideas that were helpful to the women and would not end up shifting them into undesirable situations for the sake of male inmates. Wallman shared that it would be great to move women to a facility closer to Des Moines. However, he also emphasized that any relocation could result in the loss of trained staff that were currently delivering the services to women in Rockwell City.[207]

Shortly thereafter, a commission was assembled to study the current correctional system and determine what changes might be needed. The facilities and their operations continued to be a topic of interest in the legislature, and the commission was directed to look into areas such as medical treatment and rehabilitation as opposed "warehousing" prisoners. Furthermore, the commission needed to consider society's interests in reentry, victims' rights and the humanity of the inmates. Some felt that the state's correctional institutions were getting too large, and the important tasks of rehabilitation and reentry were being overshadowed by the need to manage the large numbers of people incarcerated in the system. Others, such as Governor Ray, even felt there might be a need for additional facilities and more community corrections programs to be implemented. The goal was for the commission to present its findings the following year.[208]

As the commission began the work of assessing the statewide correctional system, life continued on at the Women's Reformatory. In the spring of 1976, the women experienced another improvement at the institution— the implementation of a new program aimed at helping them maintain strong relationships with their children during their period of incarceration. A former inmate, Carolyn Moon, started the American Friends Service

Committee (AFSC), which filled the role of helping organize visits and provide transportation for visitations between mothers and their children. At the time, over half of the seventy women in custody at Rockwell City were mothers, and many worried that their children might feel unloved during their absence. One inmate shared that the location of the facility, in comparison to where her daughter was staying with the grandmother, was too far away for the child to be brought for regular visits.[209] The program developed by Moon helped address situations such as hers. Not only did the location affect the practicality of visits, but a lack of visits could also put a strain on the relationships post-release. Such a strain could certainly impact the likelihood of reentry success.

The AFSC visitation program was highly praised by the assistant superintendent at the time, Mickey Denfeld, and it also received recognition from the National Study of Women's Correctional Programs for being a unique and helpful offering in the state. Moon was able to bring twelve to fifteen children to the facility each weekend, and she was able to provide services across the majority of the state. The success of the program was marveled, but like other unique opportunities offered at the women's facility, it was in danger of running out of funding. The program did not use state funds, and if money ran out, the program would end.[210]

Women at Rockwell City benefitted from the kindness and support of various individuals and agencies who were committed to their success, even if the state continued to limit its level of support. There were, however, some small gains in the facility that were made possible through some state funding. Perhaps surprisingly, the inmates at the reformatory were allowed to attend church services in the local Rockwell City community, so the chapel at the institution was largely unused. Superintendent Wallman was able to use the space to install equipment for a shirt factory to sew men's work shirts and contribute to the prison industry division in the state. The work shirts were designed to be sold to other nonprofit state industries, and the women were paid thirty cents per hour for their work.[211]

A few women likely benefited from the income and work experience offered by the new shirt factory, and others also saw personal growth through programs designed to address their academic progress. The library at the reformatory boasted a high usage rate of 90 percent. However, the rate of reading purportedly dropped drastically post-release.[212] Education was also available through a high school equivalency program. By 1976, the Adult Education Office at Iowa Central Community College had been offering the GED program for eight years, in addition to some college coursework.

In that time, it was reported that over one hundred women had finished the GED program, which likely increased the women's confidence, knowledge and chances of obtaining work post-release.[213]

While this series of small gains was taking place in the facility, more proposals were submitted and discarded on how to deal with overcrowding in the state's prison population and what role Rockwell City had to play in addressing the challenge. With the topic of closing the facility or relocating the women continually swirling in the background, other topics arose, such as possible shifts in the types of crimes being committed by women, security concerns and allegations of racial bias at the reformatory.

Some people suspected or claimed that women's liberation was causing a shift in the profiles of incarcerated women. In 1977, former superintendent Laurel Rans, now employed at Entropy Limited, conducted and shared the results of a study on population profiles in the facility. While Rans focused more on data sharing and interpretation as opposed to drawing ultimate conclusions, her work offered a contrasting perspective that there did not seem to be a strong correlation between the women's liberation movement and any changes in the reasons women were being incarcerated.[214]

Over the years, many had speculated that as women gained freedoms, autonomy and other advances in society, their propensity to commit more violent or typically male-dominated types of crimes would increase as well. However, some individuals and groups did not support the theory that the women's liberation movement in particular was correlated with an increase in more violent or aggressive crimes in Iowa. Crimes such as murder had only increased 1 percent since the 1920s, and assault-related incarcerations had decreased from thirty years before. The largest increases in incarcerations were seen in economic crimes, a trend that occurred before with women, and the number of women being sent to prison for forgery, embezzlement and larceny had nearly doubled since 1962. In fact, roughly 40 percent of women in the prison system were sentenced for crimes involving money-related theft or fraud.

A surge in financially motivated crimes had occurred during the Great Depression and at times when unemployment was high. This led Rans to believe that the incarceration trends of the late 1970s were once again motivated by economic need coupled with a period of tougher sentencing. Women were more often situated as heads of households and needed money to support their children. A lack of employment opportunities could put further pressure on women and essentially force them into unlawful means of supporting their families. Rans also reported that tougher sentencing was taking hold during the 1970s, which she posited was due to the politically fueled public outcries for harsher punishments. Furthermore, the women were being imprisoned for longer periods of time before earning parole.[215]

Although Rans's report paints an image of a prison population that might be docile and easy to manage, security issues increased at Rockwell City. Into the 1970s, Rockwell City remained a minimum-security facility with easily attainable furlough and no fences. According to a report in the *Des Moines Sunday Register* in 1977, 144 women had escaped at some point between the years of 1973 and 1977. By 1977, 15 of the escapees were still at large from the facility, which had a total of 80 women in custody. Many of the women who escaped did so while on furlough, and of the 15 who were still unaccounted for, 10 had left while on furlough. Some of the escapes also occurred while the women were at other state facilities, such as the Mental Health Institute at Cherokee and the hospital at the University of Iowa. Most of the women who escaped had committed economic or victimless crimes, and one of the escapees had committed a crime that was violent in nature.[216]

The escapes and security concerns became a hot topic, and multiple articles emerged profiling some of the issues people felt the facility needed to address. One issue echoed throughout multiple articles was the easiness with which furloughs from the prison could be obtained. An opinion section piece lamented how easily women were able to maintain relationships, including having sex while incarcerated, because of the availability of furloughs. The

Aerial view of the Women's Reformatory. *Courtesy of Patti Wachtendorf.*

author's concern was that men were not afforded the same opportunities, although it was pointed out that the men's facilities referenced in the piece were not minimum-security institutions like Rockwell City.[217]

Other security concerns involved the women attending college classes outside of the facility. Reports from the *Des Moines Register* claimed that women were unsupervised or under very lax supervision when attending college classes.[218] Superintendent Wallman agreed that women were not monitored the entire time they were attending classes, but instead spot-checking was used in tandem with reports on attendance from college employees. Although Wallman seemed to understand that close monitoring would be preferable, he and the Department of Social Services director, Rowland McCauley, reported that the cost to staff complete surveillance of the women while completing college coursework would be prohibitive. The two men felt that the advantages of the programs outweighed the risks at that time, so the classes were allowed to continue despite some of the security concerns that were expressed.[219]

Back at Rockwell City, further attention continued to be cast on the sexual relationships of inmates. Some were focused on sexual relations while on furlough, and others were expressing concerns about relationships with reformatory staff and other incarcerated women. Some women claimed that a cottage mother was homosexual and was selecting women to engage in inappropriate relations with her. The legislative council opened an investigation into the matter amid allegations of forced relations between staff and inmates.[220] Other inmates at the facility did not share the sentiments of those filing the complaints and felt that there might have been a concerted effort on the part of some to create the issue. A short time later, Citizens' Aide investigators deemed the allegations unfounded, although it was not the only case reviewed that year.[221]

It seems the concern, or perhaps fascination, with the sexual situations of women housed in Rockwell City was also the focus of some male inmates housed at other facilities. In one scenario, it was reported that a male inmate housed elsewhere sued Superintendent Wallman, alleging that Wallman's offering of career training opportunities to women was advancing the agenda of the women's liberation movement. The inmate claimed that his incarcerated wife began engaging in homosexual behaviors as a result.[222] The implication was that if women would not be provided such opportunities then they would not be encouraged into homosexuality. Of course, the fascination with women's sexual freedom was not new in that era, and even in modern society, it seems to be a common topic among many.

Beyond those concerned with the relationships between the women and others, individuals also reported concerns about administration for other issues, such as potentially discriminatory searches and racist language. Some reports alleged that officials engaged in discriminatory behaviors and practices with regard to Black members of the population. After receiving the reports, the Departments of Social Services and Corrections asked Citizens' Aide to look into the claims. One incident involved an official using harsh language with an inmate, and the language was interpreted to be racially motivated. Another concern that was brought forth was related to the practices of searching visitors at the facility. The investigators looked into the reports that staff were searching Black friends and family at a higher rate than White visitors. At the culmination of the investigation, Citizens' Aide concluded that there was a particular group of Black individuals associated with some of the inmates that had been caught bringing drugs into the prison. As a result, officials were only searching those individuals known to have connections to that particular drug group, and employees were not searching the Black visitors of inmates who were not associated with the drug-involved visitors.[223]

Ultimately, the investigation was not able to substantiate any reports of racism; however, it did encourage staff to be aware of how they spoke to and interacted with the women in the facility. Furthermore, Citizens' Aide advised that the practice of using the women as informants should be reconsidered. In some situations, Citizens' Aide was concerned that because the willingness to be an informant was tied to potential parole or disciplinary benefits, as well as the possible revocation of those benefits, it was a potentially unbalanced or risky situation for the women.[224]

While claims of wrongdoings by officials were not substantiated by Citizens' Aide, concerns were still cited in the study. The actions of staff were not deemed to be racist, but there was a concern about the lack of racially diverse employees at the facility. Many mentioned that it was difficult to find staff members from diverse backgrounds, due to the physical location of the facility, even though they agreed a more diverse staff would be beneficial.[225]

Although the Women's Reformatory at Rockwell City was cleared of any charges of discrimination, the Iowa Bureau of Correctional Evaluation was found to have engaged in some discriminatory practices that same year. An article in the *Des Moines Register* reported on incidents of discrimination in the ratings systems that were used for prisoners. According to reports, there had apparently been some misinterpretation in the way the rating system was written and explained, so some administrations were using race as a factor when determining the ratings of inmates. The bureau responded that this interpretation was not what it had intended and that the assessment system needed to be rewritten to correct the discrimination that was occurring as a result.[226]

Despite the tempestuous picture of life at the reformatory that some of the sensational articles painted, the everyday comings and goings were actually much milder than one might imagine. Women were allowed to keep many of their belongings after intake, including clothing and perfumes. Family members were able to bring in gifts, such as during holidays, and women continued to enjoy relative freedom throughout the facility and in private bedrooms.

One woman, Sharon, reflected on her first days of incarceration. Her prior images of prison were only what she had seen on television, and she shared with the *Muscatine Journal* that she was fearful during her first days. After her conviction for killing her ex-husband in a bar, she had been driven the two hundred miles to the reformatory by her local sheriff and his wife. This type of scenario is one commonly heard among women incarcerated during this time period. Another inmate incarcerated during a similar period reflected on the local sheriff stopping at a diner to have a meal with her prior to arriving at the Women's Reformatory.

One of Sharon's frightening interactions was when she was approached by a woman who she felt looked scary. She then realized the woman was actually quite nice. The first evening of her confinement, Sharon went to the bay in her cottage, which was a lounge with a television. The women in the bay worked hard to make her feel better about her situation. Aside from finding the facility to be a much friendlier environment than expected, Sharon was also able to attend a beauty school outside the prison grounds. The prison staff provided transportation for her to attend, and she was able to participate in the program six days a week. She reported that she had already been offered a position in a department store beauty salon on her release.[227]

The Women's Reformatory continued to provide a number of opportunities for women like Sharon, and Superintendent Ted Wallman played a significant role while at the facility, including expanding the educational offerings to ultimately include the ability to obtain a bachelor's degree. After many accomplishments and nearly ten years at the facility, in October 1979, Wallman announced his resignation.[228]

It is interesting to note that around the time of his resignation, and despite the gains Wallman had made at the facility, he still had a smaller salary than his counterparts at the men's correctional facilities by a little over $1,000.

In even greater contrast, Assistant Superintendent Margaret Denfeld, made over $5,000 less than her male counterparts at men's facilities in the state. Furthermore, most male employees at any men's facility, despite their role, earned a higher salary than Denfeld.[229]

Eight months after Wallman announced he was leaving Rockwell City, Susan M. Hunter, then twenty-nine-years-old, was hired as the next superintendent of the Women's Reformatory at a salary nearly $3,000 higher than what Wallman's had been. Hunter's background included research on correctional systems in Europe, she had been an officer and supervisor of counselors at a correctional institution in Arizona, she had conducted training of prison personnel and she was a consultant for the American Medical Association, Center for Women and Policy Studies in Washington, D.C. According to an article in the *Fort Dodge Messenger*, she was also the recipient of a Woodrow Wilson national fellowship, as well as a Law Enforcement Assistant Administration (LEAA) fellowship for researching women in the criminal justice system.[230]

As Susan Hunter transitioned into the Women's Reformatory, she took up the mantle that many of her predecessors had shouldered. What continued to persevere was a public and media conception that was often contradictory and not rooted in reality. On one hand, reports continued to circulate that women were committing more violent crimes, such as murder, and that appropriate security precautions and punishments were needed in such scenarios. However, the reality was that oftentimes the women incarcerated for murder and violent crimes were not the ones presenting security issues inside the reformatory. While the public voiced concerns with these potentially "risky" inmates, they did not follow their voice with their actions. Women's institutions continued to be funded at disproportionately lower rates than men's, and little if any consideration was given to the fact that incarcerated women often had additional expenses not as prevalent in male institutions. The vast majority of incarcerated women were mothers, and many needed greater access to job training because of their limited options on the outside. Some people seemed to assume that women, by the nature of their atavistically designated gender role, would be cared for on their release, which was often not the case. Women increasingly found themselves responsible for the financial liability of their families, yet were not provided the same opportunities to procure an income as men.

More likely, the concerns cast toward the facility at Rockwell City were less about the women held in that reformatory and more about the scenario the state and funding levels were creating. The state prison ombudsman warned that the facility was overcrowded and understaffed. There were seventeen guards responsible for around the clock care and supervision of nearly one hundred inmates. In the evenings, there was one guard per cottage of thirty-five women, and one watchman walked the grounds until three o'clock in the morning. The reformatory was averaging more than one escape a month, which was not a surprise, given the sometimes incredibly low staffing levels.[231]

Overcrowding, limited staffing and a lack of access to necessary resources caused strain and struggle in the reformatory. As a result of the overcrowding, in some cases, beds were moved into day rooms and offices. Although the limited staff members faced growing responsibilities as more women continued to arrive in Rockwell City, they were not compensated for the additional work. The lack of resources made the work environment not only more difficult, but it also increased the potential for danger. Exacerbating the risk was the fact that there was limited training for staff, and no one at the facility held the responsibility as a training officer. As resources grew thin and ratios increased, medical services were lacking, and there was no infirmary to allow prison officials to separate those with contagious illnesses from the rest of the population. Additionally, the inmates saw limits in job training and entertainment options, both of which were not only beneficial to the women but also helped occupy their time and thus kept them out of trouble during incarceration. Women were required to complete six "contact hours" a day, but options were limited to work, crafts and activities such as Alcoholics Anonymous, Narcotics Anonymous, Bible study and watching television. Only GED, clerical and welding classes were available at this time, and there were limited vocational education classes that could help women gain employment after release. The women's ability to maintain and improve their health and fitness was also limited by the absence of adequate exercise facilities.[232]

The lack of opportunities, staff, training and facilities was unfortunate in and of itself. Adding further frustrations to the situation was the fact that incarcerated men often did receive such opportunities and resources during this time. Throughout the history of corrections in Iowa, it was frequently the case that men were afforded opportunities not offered to women, so it might not have been surprising that the disparity continued into the 1980s. The ombudsman, Ray Cornell, cited that he felt "the reformatory is ripe for an equal protection lawsuit. Just compare services available to males and it's not hard to see that females come out on the bottom of the totem pole."[233]

As it turned out, Cornell's prediction was correct, and in November 1980, the Iowa Civil Liberties Union filed a federal lawsuit aimed at improving the resources available to the women incarcerated in the reformatory. According to the *Fort Dodge Messenger*, the lawsuit "alleges the Iowa prison system discriminates against the women inmates in the fields of education, job training and facilities for physical training." The plaintiff identified in the case was a thirty-three-year-old inmate serving a ten-year sentence for delivery of a controlled substance.[234]

Less than a year into Hunter's tenure, she found herself standing where many superintendents before her had stood. Once again, calls came in for the possible closure of the Women's Reformatory at Rockwell City. In the spring of 1981, the Iowa Department of Social Services presented a plan that the women in the facility be relocated to the Iowa State Training School in Mitchellville. In this case, the proposal was written with the intent of benefiting the women by moving them to a metropolitan location, which would provide more opportunities for work and education.[235] The downside of this proposal was that it would require relocating the juvenile girls housed in that metropolitan-adjacent facility at that time, essentially providing benefits for one group of women while removing those same benefits from another group.

By the spring of the following year, 1982, the proposal passed both the Iowa House and Senate. Some, such as Hunter, saw the impending move to Mitchellville as a win for the women. The facility offered the increased availability of recreational facilities, and the proximity to the state capital afforded the women additional prospects in their employment and training opportunities that were not available in the same scale at Rockwell City. Once again, it was hard to ignore another reality of the situation. The facility the women were leaving in Rockwell City was going to be converted to a facility for men. The arrival of incarcerated men would come with two additional cottages, the possibility of a new recreation building, an almost doubling of staff and a fence around the entire facility. All the same improvements had been called for when women were in the facility, yet such advances would not be made until the reformatory was inhabited by men.[236]

5

IOWA CORRECTIONAL INSTITUTION FOR WOMEN, MITCHELLVILLE, IOWA

I n 1982, twenty women sent as part of the first wave of relocation, accompanied by the assistant superintendent's dog, Taffy, arrived at the new women's prison in Mitchellville. The site of the former Girls Industrial School underwent few renovations in preparation for the women, including some updated kitchen facilities, an exercise yard, officers' stations and some painting and repair work. The women were greeted by a small, four-foot fence at the entrance. Before the relocation, Mitchellville City Council voted down a proposal to request a taller fence from the state. While Mitchellville residents, nearly a third of them volunteers at the former Girls School, were upset about the school's conversion to an adult prison, they expressed relief and some degree of comfort that it would be a prison for women instead of men. Governor Robert Ray had left it up to the legislature to decide if it wanted to transfer men or women to the Girls School in an effort to reduce overcrowding in men's prisons across the state.[237]

Although the location was new to them, the nearly sixty relocated women retained some of their Rockwell City comforts. At this time, the women were still allowed to bring their own clothes, they could add their own decorations to their rooms and the honor unit was allowed monthly outings to restaurants, movies, events and museums. There were no limits on visitors or phone calls, and it was reported that, initially, visitors could even enter the units and join the women during off-campus trips. The women brought with them the playground equipment that had been at Rockwell City, and their children could play on it in designated areas during visits. Along with many of the traditions and physical possessions, the women were also accompanied in the move by Superintendent Susan Hunter.[238]

The Iowa Correctional Institution for Women (ICIW) sat on sixty-seven acres, and the structures it inherited from the Girls School included four housing units, one medium-security lockup unit, an administration building, a powerhouse, one unoccupied building and storage buildings. The top floor of the administration building housed a library and law library that were sources of pride for the inmates who boasted of five hundred checkouts a month. Women could have personal televisions, humidifiers, alarm clocks, radios, curling irons and blow dryers, fans, personal razors, desk lamps, tape players, typewriters, sewing machines, ashtrays, plants, luggage, bedding, ice chests, jewelry, video games and lights. Women could also have up to fourteen different pairs of jeans; slacks and shorts; sixteen tops, such as sweatshirts, sweaters and blouses; and a number of other assorted clothing items, such as various coats, shoes, belts, hats, dress outfits, swimsuits and more. Children could stay for lunch with their mothers, and inmates could make two fifteen-minute phone calls per day.[239]

By the fall of 1984, Hunter reported the average population of female inmates was sixty-five, which was the lowest it had been since 1980. The women ranged in ages from seventeen to sixty-two, and the average age was twenty-nine. It was reported that 57 percent of the women were incarcerated for property offenses, 30 percent for violent offenses and 10 percent for drug offenses. The average daily cost per resident was $55, and the state budget allocation for the institution was $2,270,986. Of that budget, $50,000 was used for education and vocational training.[240]

Guards were called correctional officers, Superintendent Hunter was called Susan and neither the officers nor Susan carried weapons. Hunter shared that she never felt in danger at her work, and she was more concerned that an officer might instinctively fire a weapon and hurt an inmate than she was worried that an inmate would hurt one of them. The environment that Hunter maintained came across to some as more humane and one where inmates felt comfortable communicating one-on-one with those in charge. That said, Hunter balanced her niceness with a clear code of authority that included strict rules. Her goals for the institution were to provide a safe and supportive environment for the women, safety for the surrounding community and programming and services to help the women reenter society. Hunter remained the superintendent of the facility until December 1984, when she left for a federal appointment as a prison specialist for the National Institute of Corrections.[241]

The names used to refer to the guards and the superintendent were not the only aspects of the institution that led to frequent speculation about what life was like inside the facility. A common comment made about ICIW, even decades years later, was that the facility looked like a college campus with plenty of green space, redbrick buildings, few bars and no security fence. Some visitors and residents were concerned that it was too nice and comfortable of an environment, while others understood that, despite appearances, it was still very much a prison. What looked like women free-roaming around the facility were actually coordinated movements with officers radioing to each other every time a woman left one area to head to another. The inmates were required to engage in work and programming throughout the week, and they were subject to constant monitoring, including unit searches, drug tests and myriad rules and regulations.[242]

In addition to the many common prison practices, women at Mitchellville also faced continued challenges accessing treatment, programming and opportunities to maintain their relationships with their families and friends. Throughout the history of the Mitchellville facility, opportunities for women to grow personally and professionally through formal programming would ebb and flow. In the 1980s, women were required to maintain thirty-six hours of work, education and vocational training.

For forty-one to seventy-five cents an hour, depending on the job, the women provided a significant portion of the labor force needed to run the facility. The inmates were responsible for cleaning, meal preparation and routine maintenance, and they worked in the library, ceramics area, print shop, bindery and garment factory. Any restitution payments or court costs were automatically taken out of their earnings, and they could use any remaining funds to buy personal care items. In addition to the work requirements, the prison offered adult basic education courses and two vocational training courses through the local community college. Educational opportunities were important, as the incarcerated women had an eighth grade reading level and fifth grade math level on average. A four-week-long Women and Work class was also offered, which allowed opportunities to explore career goals and learn how to be part of the workforce.[243]

Programming opportunities and grants were sometimes available to help women work through personal struggles and maintain relationships. Half of the women came from families with histories of substance abuse, and many women had struggles themselves. Seventy-one percent of the women incarcerated in 1984 were mothers, and 31 percent were married. To help these individuals, programs were available in areas such

The laundry room in the original facility. *Photo by Alyssa Jensen.*

A partial view of the kitchen in the original Iowa Correctional Institution for Women (ICIW). *Photo by Alyssa Jensen.*

A portion of the visiting room in the original ICIW facility. *Photo by Alyssa Jensen.*

Unit 5, built when the site was occupied by the Girls School and has since been demolished. *Photo by Alyssa Jensen.*

as counseling, families and relationships, substance abuse, recreation and religion. Volunteers also supported programs and interacted with the women, and local organizations provided grants and individuals to help drive children to visit their mothers.[244] Volunteers and community organizations often played a critical role in attempting to fill some of the treatment and programming gaps created by insufficient funding for these purposes from the state legislature.

Another frequent challenge for prison officials and inmates alike was that because the prison was the only one for women, all security levels had to be managed safely and effectively in one institution. When the prison transitioned from Rockwell City to Mitchellville, unit no. 5 was identified as the security unit for the facility. Inmate movement was restricted in the unit, which contained six lockup cells on the first floor. This was the only unit at the prison with bars on the windows and locks on the doors. Women in the first-floor lockup cells took meals from trays slid through door slots, were let out three times a week to shower and received one hour of exercise per day. The second floor held some additional lower security lockup cells and was also used for new resident orientation. To be released from the security unit, women would have to receive a certain number of points collected from daily ratings by correctional officers.[245]

Shortly after the transition to the new facility and after Hunter's departure, the prison began to experience increased concerns regarding sexual relationships between officers and inmates. Court battles were fought throughout the 1970s over what sex an officer had to be to guard prisoners at gendered institutions. A 1972 amendment to Title VII prohibited employment discrimination based on sex in public as well as private sector institutions, which resulted in more men working as correctional officers in women's prisons nationwide. As one might expect, the introduction of male officers with access and sightlines to the women's daily living and cleaning spaces led to a number of sexual assault and rape allegations, some confirmed and others not. The new superintendent of the women's facility at Mitchellville, Barbara Olk Long, found herself navigating numerous sexual assault lawsuits, questions about the numbers of inmate grievances filed and concerns regarding access to treatment and substance abuse support.

The sexual assault allegations that began to dominate much of Iowa's media attention in the late 1980s caused significant challenges for inmates, prison officials, the Department of Corrections and the guards' union. At greatest risk were inmates who could be victims of sexual assault or coercion and might fear harm or repercussion from filing reports. Just like anyone else in the facility, corrections officers also stood the risk of being accused of an assault they did not commit. Prison officials and corrections leaders found themselves struggling to uncover the truth and address situations, and the guards' union fought to ensure officers' rights were being maintained when on duty and during investigations.

While the majority of sexual assault allegations came from ICIW, the high number of grievances that caught the attention of the Iowa State Bar Association were occurring throughout the entire state. A study showed that Iowan inmates were filing ten times the number of grievances as their counterparts in Minnesota and that 40 percent of all civil suits filed in Iowa's federal courts were brought by inmates. The majority of the grievances cited a lack of corrections funding, although one state official responded that the volume was simply due to a lack of respect for what he felt was one of the best grievance systems in the nation. His sentiment was not shared by all officials in the field. In response, the state Bar Association recommended more full-time lawyers be hired to represent prisoners, a review of the grievance system and additional funding for the Iowa correctional system.[246]

One of many areas where a lack of funding and resources was hurting Iowa's prison population, and women in particular, was substance abuse treatment and support. The war on drugs and associated long mandatory minimum sentences for drug crimes were filling prisons nationally, and by 1989, 85 percent of the women incarcerated in ICIW were identified as having substance abuse problems. The treatment and resources available at Mitchellville included assessment and referral, Alcoholics Anonymous, Narcotics Anonymous, group activities, counseling and education; however, the treatment was often inadequate. In some cases, treatment was unavailable for newer types of addictions. Additionally, the facility often struggled to find enough beds for women in community substance abuse programs. Fewer female than male substance abusers often meant that some drug programs were not profitable or even sustainable for women, so the majority of available facilities were for men only. Although women represented the minority of the substance abuse population, the consequences could often be greater for themselves and for society. The babies of mothers with addictions were often born addicted themselves. Children entering homes with substance abuse problems faced neglect, risk of engaging in substance abuse, domestic violence, the need of public assistance and increased criminal activity.[247]

As ICIW faced many challenges in Iowa's correctional system, the steady ascent in the number of incarcerated women would continue to be a significant issue. By 1989, the facility was holding 163 women in a facility designed for 123.[248] By 1991, that number reached 180.[249] By 2007, the population breached 600.[250] As the number of inmates accelerated, calls for expanded or new facilities were renewed. In the summer of 1990, the Iowa Board of Corrections approved a $17 million plan that would create space for 456 more inmates statewide, in addition to a plan already supported by the legislature to add 522 more beds. The state's inmate population was 800 people over capacity, and requests for expansion included new beds for most of the men's prisons, as well as ICIW. In total, $2.3 million was requested to add forty-eight more two-person rooms at the Mitchellville facility. Additionally, a proposal was made that included plans for a new 630-bed facility for men in Newton, Iowa.[251]

In the fall of 1991, perhaps as a result of overcrowding and other grievances, the attorney general convened a committee to hold hearings and facility visits to assess the situation. In her statement following her first few weeks of visits she stated, "Overcrowding has been a consistent theme.... Our criminal sentencing options are largely determined by the amount of space available in our prisons." She concluded that overcrowding made it nearly impossible to offer programming to improve inmates' chances of success on reentry to society.[252] The conclusions of the committee were echoed by community members and inmates, and some thoughts were shared the following spring at a Brown Bag Forum held by the Coalition for Prison Reform. One inmate spoke about loss of identity while incarcerated. A longtime ICIW volunteer reflected on how much regression she had seen in programming. She mentioned that the population of women had significantly increased during her volunteering years, yet there were still only the same two counseling positions for 185 women, while they used to serve closer to 100 women. Prison officials echoed agreement with the lack of counseling and lamented the inadequate state funding needed to hire more staff. In addition to insufficient funds for treatment and programming, others added that overcrowding was leading to shorter sentences and early releases to help lower the populations, which often meant women were released before they could finish programming.[253]

Despite scarce treatment funding, many reentry programs were supported by volunteers and community organizations. Lutheran Social Services of Iowa facilitated a Match-2 program since the 1970s, which partnered community volunteers with inmates in the hopes that long-term friendships would develop and volunteers could act as a support system for women after transitioning back to the outside.[254] Between 1972 and 1992, the program matched more than two hundred women, and by 1988, only 3 percent of the women who participated were incarcerated again.[255] Lutheran Social Services continued to provide additional support initiatives over the years, including the largely popular Storybook Project introduced by Betty Trost, a private consultant in family and consumer sciences. The organization, as well as prison officials, understood the value of incarcerated mothers maintaining relationships with their children, and the project gave women the opportunity to record themselves reading stories to their children on cassette tapes. Advocates of the program touted its ability to improve relationships, the odds of success post-release, literacy and the chances of children doing better in school and enjoying reading.[256]

The state also provided some support by developing inmate work crews tasked with taking on community service type projects. A $170,000 pilot program was modeled after a similar program in Minnesota and was designed to give inmates with good records and nearing release an opportunity to gain skills, earn money and perhaps prepare a bit more for their transition out of the facility.[257] The volunteer and work programs were helpful, but there were not enough opportunities to meet the needs of the institution. Furthermore, the piecemeal introduction of new programs could not resolve the continued rapid ascent of incarceration rates promulgated by Nixon's war on drugs, followed by Reagan and Congress's passage and support of mandatory minimums for drug sentences in 1986.[258] Between 1988 and 1994, the statewide prison population rose from 2,886 to 4,973, and the budget increased from $55.7 million to $89.7 million. In 1982, there were 77 individuals sent to prison for drugs in the state, and by 1993, that number rose to 529.[259] Not only did these anti-drug laws drastically increase the prison population, but they also included discriminatory sentencing guidelines to disproportionately incarcerate Black citizens.[260]

In the early 1990s, construction plans moved forward at ICIW, and new facilities were opened, including a fifty-bed housing unit, a sixty-bed violator and drug treatment unit, a new kitchen and dining area and new laundry and medical facilities.[261] Another change that came around the same time is that Superintendent Barb Olk Long began to be referred to as warden. Perhaps another sign that times were changing was that in 1993, a twelve-foot fence with razor wire was added around the perimeter of the prison for the first time in the history of women-only institutions in Iowa.[262]

The capacity of the institution was increased to 233, and 217 women were incarcerated by 1993. That year, 67.0 percent of Mitchellville's inmate population were White, and 30.0 percent were Black.[263] The statewide Black population that same year was around 2.4 percent.[264] By 1997, the racial

A cell in the now mostly demolished original facility. A second set of bunk beds occupies the same room. *Photo by Alyssa Jensen.*

disparities gained attention in the media and started to become the topic of state taskforces. Dean Wright, professor of sociology at Drake University, who had also been a member of Attorney General Bonnie Campbell's Committee on Criminal Sentencing in the early 1990s, was quoted in the *Des Moines Register*, saying, "Our justice system is very racist." An Equality in the Courts taskforce further concluded "that for each of the three aspects of criminal case processing—charging, pretrial release and sentencing—there is evidence of disparate treatment associated with race."[265]

Over the next couple of years, the population jumped again from 233 to 330 at ICIW. Another 21 women were in the parole and work release violation program, and 51 women were held at the Iowa Medical and Classification Center in Oakdale. Along with the population increase spurred by the war on drugs, the state Citizens' Aide office indicated that there was also a national movement to be tough on crime, with an increased emphasis on punishment for both men and women. As in the past, many women were still overwhelming incarcerated for crimes such as forgery, bad check writing and prostitution, but the numbers of women incarcerated for more violent crimes continued to rise as well. By 1995, the number one reason for incarceration was forgery, followed by drugs and then theft.[266] In a couple short years, the number of women incarcerated at ICIW continued to climb to 525, and to deal with overcrowding, 100 women were moved to other prisons outside of Iowa. The move was a short-term solution while additional prison expansion projects at Mitchellville were completed.[267]

By 2000, significant progress was made on construction at the existing ICIW facility. Eight years before, inmates had filed a federal class action lawsuit about their unequal treatment and facilities compared to men, and although that lawsuit was struck down, the corrections director in 2000, W.L. "Kip" Kautzky, was quoted in the paper, saying, "Had we not done this, we would be under a federal court order."[268] Federal court orders had occurred in other facilities, such as in 2002, when a federal judge ordered changes to how mentally ill men were housed in Fort Madison, which further highlights the perpetual lack of funding and support from the state legislature to provide fair and equitable correctional environments desired by both inmates and prison officials.[269]

The improvements to the women's facility in 2000 included a new 184-bed dormitory, progress on a 48-bed maximum-security unit, a security fence, an industries building and a heating plant. A chapel was added by 2002, and eighty-one new employees were hired, including twenty new counselors.[270] In addition to the new buildings, this phase of the prison's history also included a new warden in 1999, Diann Wilder-Tomlinson, the first Black warden at the Iowa Correctional Institution for Women. Wilder-Tomlinson's background included leading the Iowa Civil Rights Commission, work as a Department of Corrections administrative law judge and assistant director of legal and policy issues, and experience in the army as a legal clerk and court reporter.[271]

Alongside some of the improvements in the physical facilities came some gains in the programming and treatment options for women. The ebbing and flowing in availability of such activities plagued the women's prison system from its earliest days and would continue to do so well into the beginning of the twenty-first century. Sometimes programs were developed in the sole interest of those incarcerated, and at other times, the programs were designed to help the women while also addressing a challenge faced by the state or other institution. For example, 2000 was a period of low unemployment in the state, and employers were challenged to find new workers. This is a scenario that would play out again two decades later. Employers began turning to the prison population to fill jobs, and job fairs were offered for inmates nearing release and former inmates.[272]

Community groups and private organizations brought additional programming opportunities and volunteers to the prison, such as Marti Sivi, who led a prison drama project paid for by Sivi herself and a $10,538 grant from the Chrysalis Foundation. Dean Wright, sociology professor, evaluated the program and found that it was raising self-worth and self-esteem among the inmate participants. The program provided role models, encouraged teamwork, taught skills and demonstrated nonthreatening ways to express emotion.[273] More programs were also started to enhance and support the mother and child relationship, in addition to the book project that was still being facilitated by Lutheran Social Services. Of the 560 women in ICIW at the time, 65 percent had dependent children. Opportunities for mothers included a three-month program designed to teach women how to manage their money, free time and relationships. Participants were able to be with their children once a month on the prison grounds for three hours. For the incarcerated women who had children but did not have parental rights, a mail program provided them the opportunity to write letters or draw pictures for their children.[274]

Other external support and training opportunities included diversity training that was provided by the Gay and Lesbian Resource Center for inmates and staff, and business classes with handicrafts sales opportunities were facilitated and financially funded through a $50,000 grant from the

Ms. Foundation.[275] Internal programs and activities included education courses, support groups, library services, religious programs and recreation options, such as gym time, T-shirt painting and sewing.[276] One of the most exciting programs for many women at the facility was the Pets and Women Succeeding, or PAWS Program, which was coordinated with the Animal Rescue League of Iowa (ARL). Women who were without disciplinaries for six months could request to take on dogs that needed some additional socialization and training.[277]

Over the next few years, the overall environment at ICIW remained fairly stable, with some continued cycling of new treatment programs and activities. The next substantial change on the horizon would be its final change of such magnitude in the prison's current history. Around 2007, conversations began regarding the number of beds needed to house the still increasing numbers of women being incarcerated in the state. Mitchellville currently held 622 women, and 100 more were in the prison unit at the Mount Pleasant Correctional Facility and the state's prison reception center at Oakdale. The state was predicting more than another 200 women would be added to that number in ten more years.[278] Calls continued for more preventative measures and community-based corrections programs to try to decrease the number of women sent to prison. Unfortunately, similar calls had occurred unanswered for decades, and the decision was made to build a completely new prison for women on ICIW's grounds that could hold the entire state's female population for years to come.

The legislature approved $199 million in funds for prison construction at both Fort Madison and Mitchellville, and officials indicated that they hoped for the new facility at ICIW to be complete by 2012. Once again, legislative officials cited one reason for moving ahead with these projects, despite a significant budget shortfall, was the fear of a federal civil rights lawsuit because of living conditions at the existing facilities.[279] At the time, many of the women in Mitchellville were still living in units designed for the former Girls School, and several buildings were in various states of deterioration due to age or simply did not meet the needs of a modern prison environment.

By 2013, almost all of the new $68 million facility was finished, and offenders were scheduled to start moving into the new buildings by winter. According to the prison's warden at the time, Patti Wachtendorf, the new prison was designed to complement a "softer, gentler" approach to women's corrections. The buildings that were constructed during this time are the facilities used and inhabited by the women at the time of this writing. The new administration building includes large windows, an open atrium and an

A children's play area in the visiting room of the new ICIW facility. *Photo by Alyssa Jensen.*

One wing of the new general population unit. *Photo by Alyssa Jensen.*

The new health unit as it was nearing completion in 2013. *Photo by Alyssa Jensen.*

impressively large visiting area for women and their families. Additionally, the administration facility houses master control operations, security offices, a training room, a staff wellness area and locker rooms. A new general population building has four wings and includes beds for 256 offenders. Included in the building is a medication and triage room, laundry facilities, classrooms, offices and computers for offenders. Across the yard is a health services building, which holds orientation cells, hospice, assisted living, medical recovery, acute and subacute areas and special needs areas. The health services building also houses the prison's health care, dental and optometry spaces. Inside the programs building, offenders are able to use the gymnasium, education classrooms, HiSET testing center, the craft room, the hair care area and the library. Finally, the new construction included the completion of a new food services building, which was designed with two separate dining areas for increased efficiency and to provide the ability to separate groups or populations as needed.[280]

The new facility represents significant progress for Iowa's incarcerated women. In fact, it is one of the most significant endeavors taken on their behalf by the state in the over 150 year history of women's corrections. However, such a development is not without challenges. The former college-like and homey environments women experienced in the original

An exterior view of the new general population unit. *Photo by Alyssa Jensen.*

Mitchellville facility and at Rockwell City were only memories and had been replaced by an attractive and nature-rooted yet highly modernized and more institutional-looking prison environment. Personal furnishings, clothing and even the occasional trips into town with family, which provided at least moments of not feeling "locked-up," were officially gone for many of the women still incarcerated in 2013 who once lived at the original ICIW site and a few who had even lived in the Rockwell City Reformatory.

As of this writing, the transition to the new facility is still in the recent past, and it naturally remains to be seen what the future has in store for Iowa's incarcerated women. What is clear, however, is that the fight for criminal justice and corrections reform is not over for correctional leaders and incarcerated individuals. In 2020, state institutions are still underfunded, and incarcerated individuals continue to face significant hurdles on release. Until August 5, 2020, Iowa remained the only state in the country to deny formerly incarcerated individuals voting rights for life.[281] Due to an executive order, some rights have been restored, but these could easily be overturned by a future governor without action from the state legislature to change state law. Further refusing to support practices known to increase successful reentry, Pell Grant educational funding accessibility has not been fully restored to incarcerated individuals outside a few Second Chance Pell pilot programs. In Iowa, those pilot programs were not approved for the district that holds ICIW, and therefore, women might have reduced access to the current Second Chance Pell program.[282] On top of these state-specific issues, Iowan women, as well as women all over the country, continue to face numerous uphill battles, such as the fights to dismantle systemic racism in all aspects of the criminal justice system, find safe and equitable solutions for LGBTQ+ appropriate incarceration options and gain access to truly impactful prevention and reentry programs.

Over the history of women's corrections, passionate and driven corrections officials, incarcerated individuals and community members and organizations have led charges and influenced movements to bring about change and hope. There are countless individuals who continue to carry those mantles today. At the Iowa Correctional Institution for Women, Warden Sheryl Dahm has endorsed the use of "gender-responsive corrections," which is designed on the premise that prison rules were originally created with violent men in mind and that women might benefit from a different approach. Women sometimes enter prison through different pathways than men, and they can also experience different types of victimization themselves prior to their incarceration.[283] Incarcerated individuals at Mitchellville are also an area of focus at multiple local colleges, such as longtime partner Des Moines Area Community College. These institutions are committed to helping women access currently available education programs as well as increasing educational options and opportunities. With the support of such individuals and institutions, the women's correctional system in Iowa will likely continue to make forward progress. However, plenty of challenges still lie ahead, and systemic change will not come as quickly as incarcerated individuals, corrections officials and communities deserve.

NOTES

Epigraph

1. Committee on the Judiciary, United States Congress, *Juvenile Delinquency: National, Federal, and Youth-Serving Agencies* (Washington, D.C.: U.S. Government Printing Office, 1954).

Chapter 1

2. Iowa Pathways, "Iowa History Timeline: Text Version," Iowa Public Television, http://www.iowapbs.org.
3. Patrick J. Jung, "Lonely Sentinel: A Military History of Fort Madison, 1808–1813," *Annals of Iowa* 75, no. 3 (2016): 201–33.
4. Iowa Pathways, "Iowa History Timeline."
5. Captain J.W. Campbell, "Fragmentary History of the Fort Madison Penitentiary," *Bulletin of Iowa Institutions* (1900): 171–8.
6. Ibid., 172.
7. Board of Inspectors of the Iowa Penitentiary, *Report of the Board of Inspectors of the Iowa State Penitentiary for the Two Years Ending First of Oct., 1859* (Des Moines, IA: GPO, 1859), 211–27.
8. State of Iowa Department of Justice, *The Report of the Committee Appointed to Investigate the Character of the Warden and the General Management of the Iowa Penitentiary at Fort Madison together with a Report Concerning the Jail System of Iowa with Recommendations* (Des Moines, IA: GPO, 1912).

9. Board of Inspectors of the Iowa Penitentiary, *Report of the Board of Inspectors of the Iowa State Penitentiary for the Two Years Ending First of Oct., 1857.*

10. Honorary P. Inskeep, warden, Board of Inspectors of the Iowa Penitentiary, *Report of the Board of Inspectors of the Iowa State Penitentiary for the Two Years Ending First of Oct., 1859* (Des Moines, IA: GPO, 1859), 6.

11. Board of Inspectors of the Iowa Penitentiary, *Report Oct., 1857.*

12. Seth H. Craig, warden, *Biennial Report of the Warden of the Penitentiary to the Governor* (Des Moines, IA: GPO, 1877), 7–10.

13. Ibid., 45–6.

14. E.C., McMillan, warden, *Biennial Report of the Warden of the Penitentiary to the Governor* (Des Moines, IA: GPO, 1881), 5.

15. Lovina B. Benedict, *Woman's Work for Woman* (Des Moines, IA: Iowa Printing Company, 1892).

16. "Lena Stanton," *Chicago Daily Tribune*, May 29, 1881.

17. *Legislative Documents Submitted to the Twentieth General Assembly of the State of Iowa, Volume 4* (Des Moines, IA: GPO, 1884).

18. "News in Brief," *Graphic* (Postville, IA), October 19, 1893.

19. Steve Wendl, "A Novel Escape," Anamosa State Penitentiary, http://www.asphistory.com.

20. "Female Convicts," *Cedar Rapids Gazette*, April 17, 1883.

21. Wendl, "Novel Escape."

22. Kerry Segrave, *Parricide in the United States, 1840–1899* (Jefferson, NC: McFarland and Company, 2009).

23. Steve Wendl, "Obituary," Anamosa State Penitentiary, http://www.asphistory.com.

24. Cyndi Banks, *Women in Prison: A Reference Handbook* (Santa Barbara, CA: ABC-CLIO, 2003).

25. Ibid., 2–3.

26. Sharon E. Wood, *The Freedom of the Streets: Work, Citizenship, and Sexuality in the Gilded Age City* (Chapel Hill: University of North Carolina Press, 2005).

27. "Charles Miller, the Woman," *San Francisco Call*, November 4, 1891.

Chapter 2

28. Board of Commissioners, *Biennial Report of the Board of Commissioners of the Additional Penitentiary to the Governor and Fifteenth General Assembly* (Des Moines, IA: GPO, 1873), 15.

29. Bertha Finn, "Iowa State Men's Reformatory: Here Since 1872," Anamosa State Penitentiary, http://www.asphistory.com.

30. Ibid.

31. A.E. Martin, *Biennial Report of the Warden of the Additional Penitentiary to the Governor and Seventeenth General Assembly* (Des Moines, IA: GPO, 1877).

32. Ibid., 21.

33. A.E. Martin, *Biennial Report of the Warden of the Additional Penitentiary to the Governor of the State* (Des Moines, IA: GPO, 1879), 22.

34. A.E. Martin, *Third Biennial Report of the Warden of the Additional Penitentiary to the Governor of the State* (Des Moines, IA: GPO, 1881).

35. S.W. Wetmore and C.L. Peterson, "Index to All Prisoners Received at Anamosa from Number One to 7552 from May 13th 1873 to January 1st 1915," 1915, PDF file, https://sites.google.com.

36. Iowa governor, *Special Message of the Governor of Iowa to the Seventeenth General Assembly, Communicating Report of Pardons and Remissions* (Des Moines, IA: GPO, 1878).

37. Eighteenth General Assembly, *Legislative Documents Submitted to the Eighteenth General Assembly of the State of Iowa* (Des Moines, IA: GPO, 1880), 13.

38. A.E. Martin, *Sixth Biennial Report of the Warden of the Additional Penitentiary to the Governor of the State* (Des Moines, IA: GPO, 1883), 6.

39. Steve Wendl, "Justifiable Homicide or Willful Murder? Domestic Violence (and its Revenge) a Century Ago," Anamosa State Penitentiary, http://www.asphistory.com.

40. Ibid.; Patricia L. Bryan and Thomas Wolf, *Midnight Assassin: A Murder in America's Heartland* (Iowa City: University of Iowa Press, 2005).

41. "John Hossack," *Iowa Cold Cases* (blog), https://iowacoldcases.org; Bryan and Wolf, *Midnight Assassin*.

42. "A Direful Tragedy: The Lenihan Women," Anamosa State Penitentiary, http://www.asphistory.com.

43. A.E. Martin, *Seventh Biennial Report of the Warden of the Additional Penitentiary to the Governor of the State* (Des Moines, IA: GPO, 1885), 8–10.

44. "A Direful Tragedy."

45. Wm. A. Hunter, *Fourteenth Biennial Report of the Warden of the Penitentiary at Anamosa, Iowa, to the Board of Control of State Institutions for the Period Ending June 30, 1899* (Des Moines, IA: GPO, 1900), 30.

46. Wm. A. Hunter, *Fifteenth Biennial Report of the Warden of the Penitentiary at Anamosa, Iowa, to the Board of Control of State Institutions* (Anamosa, IA: Prison Press, 1902), 46.

47. Ibid.

48. Wm. A. Hunter, *Sixteenth Biennial Report of the Warden of the Penitentiary at Anamosa, Iowa, to the Board of Control of State Institutions* (Anamosa, IA: Prison Press, 1903).

49. Report by the Governor of Iowa of Pardons, *Suspensions of Sentence Commutations and Remissions of Fines. From January 13, 1898, to January 10, 1900* (Des Moines, IA: B. Murphy, State Printer, 1902).

50. Ibid.

51. Marquis Barr, *The Nineteenth Biennial Report of the Warden of the Reformatory at Anamosa to the Board of Control of State Institutions* (Anamosa, IA: Reformatory Print, 1910); Charles C. McClaughry, *Twentieth Biennial Report of the Warden of the Reformatory at Anamosa, Iowa to the Board of Control of State Institutions* (Anamosa, IA: Reformatory Print, 1912).

52. Alexander W. Pisciotta, *Benevolent Repression: Social Control and the American Reformatory-Prison Movement* (New York: New York University Press, 1994).

53. McClaughry, *Twentieth Biennial Report*.

54. Ibid.

55. J.M. Baumel, *Twenty-Third Biennial Report of the Warden of the Reformatory at Anamosa, Iowa to the Board of Control of State Institutions* (Anamosa, IA: Reformatory Print, 1918).

56. J.M. Baumel, *Twenty-Fourth Biennial Report of the Warden of the Men's Reformatory, Anamosa, Iowa to the Board of Control of State Institutions* (Anamosa, IA: Men's Reformatory Print, 1920).

57. J.M. Baumel, *Twenty-Fifth Biennial Report of the Warden of the Men's Reformatory, Anamosa, Iowa to the Board of Control of State Institutions* (Anamosa, IA: Men's Reformatory Print, 1922).

Chapter 3

58. Douglas M. Wertsch, *The Girls' Reform School of Iowa, 1865–1899* (Lewiston, NY: Edwin Mellen Press, 1997).

59. Ibid., 18.

60. Ibid., 20.

61. Ibid.

62. Ibid.

63. Ibid.

64. Louis Thomas Jones, "The Quakers of Iowa," Iowa History Project, http://iagenweb.org; Wertsch, *Girls' Reform School*.

65. Jones, "Quakers of Iowa."

66. Ibid.

67. *First Biennial Report of the Trustees and Superintendent of the Iowa Reform School Situated in Lee County, to the General Assembly of the State* (Des Moines, IA: GPO, 1870).

68. *Second Biennial Report of the Trustees and Superintendent of the Iowa Reform School Situated in Lee County, to the General Assembly of the State* (Des Moines, IA: GPO, 1872).

69. Wertsch, *Girls' Reform School of Iowa.*

70. Jones, *Quakers of Iowa.*

71. *Third Biennial Report of the Trustees, Superintendent, and Treasurer of the Iowa Reform School, to the General Assembly of the State* (Des Moines, IA: GPO, 1874).

72. Ibid., 186.

73. *Fourth Biennial Report of the Board of Trustees of the Iowa Reform School, to the Governor of the State* (Des Moines, IA: GPO, 1876).

74. Ibid.

75. *Fifth Biennial Report of the Trustees, Superintendent, and Treasurer of the Iowa Reform School, to the General Assembly of the State* (Des Moines, IA: GPO, 1877).

76. *Sixth Biennial Report of the Trustees, Superintendent, and Treasurer of the Iowa Reform School, to the General Assembly of the State* (Des Moines, IA: GPO, 1880).

77. Wertsch, *Girls' Reform School.*

78. Ibid.

79. *Seventh Biennial Report of the Trustees, Superintendent, and Treasurer of the Iowa Reform School, to the General Assembly of the State* (Des Moines, IA: GPO, 1882).

80. Lois Craig, "Eminent Iowan Series," *Annals of Iowa* 31, no. 8 (1953): 564–87.

81. Wertsch, *Girls' Reform School.*

82. *Seventh Biennial Report.*

83. N. Hornyak, "Polk County, Iowa Cities and Towns," Genealogical Research in Iowa, http://frelik.homestead.com.

84. Ibid.

85. Wertsch, *Girls' Reform School.*

86. Hornyak, "Polk County."

87. Wertsch, *Girls' Reform School.*

88. Hornyak, "Polk County."

89. *Ninth Biennial Report of the Trustees of the Iowa Industrial School, Embracing Reports from the Superintendent of the Boys' Department at Eldora, the Superintendent of the Girls' Department at Mitchellville, and also the Treasurer of the Board* (Des Moines, IA: GPO, 1885).

90. Wertsch, *Girls' Reform.*

91. Ibid.
92. Ibid.
93. Ibid.
94. Ibid.
95. Ibid.
96. Ibid.
97. Ibid.
98. Ibid.
99. Ibid.
100. Ibid.
101. Ibid.
102. *Tenth Biennial Report of the Trustees of the Iowa Industrial School, Embracing Reports from the Superintendent of the Boys' Department at Eldora, the Superintendent of the Girls' Department at Mitchellville, and also the Treasurer of the Board, to the Governor of the State of Iowa, for the Fiscal Term Ending June 30, 1887* (Des Moines, IA: GPO, 1887).
103. *Souvenir History of Pella, Iowa [1847–1922]* (Pella, IA: Booster Press, 1922), 29.
104. Iowa General Assembly, *Legislative Documents Submitted to the General Assembly of the State of Iowa* (N.p: F.W. Palmer, 1866).
105. Wertsch, *Girls' Reform School*; Sharon E. Wood, "Savage Girls: The 1899 Riot at the Mitchellville Girls School," *Iowa Heritage Illustrated* 80 (Fall 1999): 108–21.
106. *Tenth Biennial Report.*
107. F.P. Fitzgerald, *Seventeenth Biennial Report of the Superintendent of the Industrial School for Girls at Mitchellville to the Board of Control of State Institutions* (Glenwood, IA: State Institution Press, 1902).
108. *Sixteenth Biennial Report of the Superintendent of the Iowa Industrial School for Girls at Mitchellville to the Board of Control of State Institutions* (Des Moines, IA: F.R. Conaway, state printer, 1899).
109. F.P. Fitzgerald, *Superintendent's Biennial Report of the Iowa State Industrial School for Girls at Mitchellville, to the Board of Control of State Institutions, for the Period Ending June 30, 1905* (N.p, 1905).
110. Wood, "Savage Girls."
111. Ibid., 113.
112. Ibid.
113. Ibid.
114. Ibid., 115.
115. Ibid., 114.

116. Ibid., 118.

117. Ibid., 118–20.

118. Ibid.

119. Ibid., 119.

120. Ibid., 120.

121. Ibid.

122. Fitzgerald, *Superintendent's Biennial Report.*

123. F.P. Fitzgerald, *Twentieth Biennial Report of the Superintendent of the Iowa Industrial School for Girls* (Mitchellville, IA, 1906).

124. Ibid.

125. F.P. Fitzgerald, *Twenty-First Biennial Report of the Superintendent of the Industrial School for Girls* (Eldora: Press of the Iowa Industrial School, 1908).

126. Hattie R. Garrison, *Twenty-Second Biennial Report of the Superintendent and the First Biennial Report of the State Agent of the Industrial School for Girls at Mitchellville, Iowa to the Board of Control of State Institution*s (Eldora, IA: Industrial School Print, 1910).

127. Wood, "Savage Girls."

128. Ibid., 120.

129. Lucy M. Sickels, *Twenty-Third Biennial Report of the Superintendent and Fourth Biennial Report of the State Agent of the Industrial School for Girls at Mitchellville, Iowa to the Board of Control of State Institutions for the Period Ending June 30, 1912* (Eldora, IA: Industrial School Print, 1912).

130. Lucy M. Sickels, *Twenty-Fourth Biennial Report of the Superintendent and Fifth Biennial Report of the State Agent of the Industrial School for Girls at Mitchellville, Iowa. To the Board of Control of State Institutions for the Period Ending June 30, 1914* (Eldora, IA: Industrial School Print, 1914).

131. Ibid.

132. Lucy M. Sickels, *Twenty-Sixth Biennial Report of the Superintendent and Seventh Biennial Report of the State Agent of the Training School for Girls Mitchellville, Iowa. To the Board of Control of State Institutions for the Period Ending June 30, 1918* (Anamosa, IA: Reformatory Print, 1918).

133. Lucy M. Sickels, *Twenty-Eighth Biennial Report of the Superintendent and Ninth Biennial Report of the State Agent of the Training School for Girls Mitchellville, Iowa* (Eldora, IA: State Training School Printing Class, 1922).

134. Ray M. Hanchett, *Twenty-Ninth Biennial Report of the Superintendent and the Tenth Biennial Report of the State Agent of the Training School for Girls Mitchellville, Iowa to the Board of Control of State Institutions* (Anamosa, IA: Men's Reformatory, 1924).

135. Ray M. Hanchett, *Thirtieth Biennial Report of the Superintendent and the Eleventh Biennial Report of the State Agent of the Training School for Girls Mitchellville, Iowa to the Board of Control of State Institutions* (Anamosa, IA: Men's Reformatory, 1926).

136. Ray M. Hanchett, *Thirty-First Biennial Report of the Superintendent and the Twelfth Biennial Report of the State Agent of the Training School for Girls Mitchellville, Iowa* (Eldora, IA: Training School for Boys Printing Class, 1928).

137. Ray M. Hanchett, *Thirty-Second Biennial Report of the Superintendent and the Thirteenth Biennial Report of the State Agent of the Training School for Girls Mitchellville, Iowa* (Eldora, IA: Training School for Boys Printing Class, 1930).

138. Ray M. Hanchett, *Thirty-Third Biennial Report of the Superintendent and the Fourteenth Biennial Report of the State Agent of the Training School for Girls Mitchellville, Iowa* (Eldora, IA: Training School for Boys Printing Class, 1932).

139. State of Iowa, *Nineteenth Biennial Report of the Board of Control of State Institutions* (Des Moines, IA: GPO, 1934).

140. State of Iowa, *Twentieth Biennial Report of the Board of Control of State Institutions* (Des Moines, IA, GPO, 1936).

141. State of Iowa, *Twenty-Second Biennial Report of the Board of Control of State Institutions* (Des Moines, IA: GPO, 1940).

142. State of Iowa, *Twenty-Fourth Biennial Report of the Board of Control of State Institutions* (Des Moines, IA: GPO, 1944).

143. State of Iowa, *Twenty-Fifth Biennial Report of the Board of Control of State Institutions* (Des Moines, IA: GPO, 1946).

144. State of Iowa, *Twenty-Seventh Biennial Report of the Board of Control of State Institutions* (Des Moines, IA: GPO, 1950).

145. Diann Wilder-Tomlinson, *Iowa Correctional Institution for Women: 2008 Annual Report* (N.p: Department of Corrections, 2008).

146. T. Meinch, "Mitchellville Was a Horror That I Lived Through," *Des Moines Register*, November 4, 2012.

147. S. Walters, "Proposes Closing Facility at Mitchellville," 1976.

148. "State's Social Services Face Budget Cutback," March 9, 1977.

149. Tony Leys, "Iowa Girls Were Abused at Wisconsin Facility after Iowa Closed Toledo School, Lawsuit Says," *Des Moines Register*, August 3, 2017.

Chapter 4

150. Lena A. Beach, *First Biennial Report of the Superintendent of the Women's Reformatory. Rockwell City, Iowa* (1918).
151. Ibid.
152. Ibid.
153. Lena A. Beach, *Second Biennial Report of the Superintendent of the Women's Reformatory. Rockwell City, Iowa* (Anamosa, IA: Reformatory Print, 1920).
154. Lena A. Beach, *Third Biennial Report of the Superintendent of the Women's Reformatory. Rockwell City, Iowa* (Anamosa, IA: Reformatory Print, 1922).
155. Laurel L. Rans, et al., *Population Profiles: Iowa Women's Reformatory 1918–1975* (Pittsburgh, PA: Entropy Limited, 1976).
156. Eleanor Hutchison, *Fourth Biennial Report of the Superintendent of the Women's Reformatory at Rockwell City, Iowa* (Anamosa, IA: Men's Reformatory Print, 1924).
157. Ibid.
158. Ibid.
159. Eleanor Hutchinson, *Fifth Biennial Report of the Superintendent of the Women's Reformatory at Rockwell City, Iowa to the Board of Control of State Institutions* (Anamosa, IA: Men's Reformatory Print, 1926).
160. Ibid.
161. Rans et al., *Population Profiles*.
162. Pauline E. Johnston, *Seventh Biennial Report of the Superintendent of the Women's Reformatory at Rockwell City, Iowa to the Board of Control of State Institutions* (Anamosa, IA: Men's Reformatory Print, 1930); Pauline E. Johnston, *Eighth Biennial Report of the Superintendent of the Women's Reformatory at Rockwell City, Iowa to the Board of Control of State Institutions* (Anamosa, IA: Men's Reformatory Print, 1932); Pauline E. Johnston, *Ninth Biennial Report of the Superintendent of the Women's Reformatory at Rockwell City, Iowa to the Board of Control of State Institutions* (Anamosa, IA: Men's Reformatory Print, 1934).
163. Dick Spry, "Iowa Prison Has No Walls, Armed Guards, or Real Bars," *Des Moines Sunday Register*, July 7, 1935; "A Picture Letter from Iowa Prison Without Bars," *Des Moines Sunday Register*, April 3, 1938.
164. "Babies Born to Women Prisoners Taken from Mothers Immediately," *Des Moines Sunday Register*, September 5, 1948; "Crime Increase Since Last War Fills Institution," *Rockwell City Advocate*, March 25, 1948.
165. William Brown, "Reformatory Happy over Warden's Tot," *Des Moines Sunday Register*, April 22, 1951.

166. U.S. Department of Justice, "Prisoners 1925–81," Washington, D.C, 1982, https://www.bjs.gov.

167. "Crime Increase Since Last War."

168. "Babies Born to Women Prisoners."

169. Rans, et al., *Population Profiles*.

170. Elda M. Kyles, "Women's Reformatory," in *Board of Control of State Institutions: Part 1. Thirty-Third Biennial Report* (State of Iowa, 1962), 56–58; Elda M. Kyles, "Document Containing Rockwell City Reformatory Rules and Guidelines for Employees."

171. Kyles, "Document Containing Rockwell City."

172. Ibid.

173. Ibid.

174. "Babies Born to Women Prisoners."

175. Kyles, "Women's Reformatory"; Kyles, "Document Containing Rockwell City."

176. Kyles, "Women's Reformatory."

177. Ibid.

178. Ibid.

179. George Mills, "Law Requires Female Head of Women's Reformatory," *Des Moines Register*, July 11, 1966.

180. "Expenses at the Reformatory Rose 27.3% During 1967."

181. "Dee Allen, 72, Indianola," *Des Moines Register*, June 15, 2018.

182. Helen Weiershauser, "Reformatory Life Has Improved, but It Still Is a Painful Experience," *Muscatine Journal*, April 12, 1969.

183. Ibid.

184. Ibid.

185. Helen Weiershauser, "Youthful Administrator Heads Staff of 44 Women at Women's Reformatory," *Muscatine Journal*, April 17, 1969.

186. Weiershauser, "Reformatory Life Has Improved."

187. Helen Weiershauser, "Women Inmates Learn a Trade and Some Are on Work-Release Programs," *Muscatine Journal*, April 16, 1969.

188. Helen Weiershauser, "Inmates at Half-Way House Experience a New Way of Life," *Muscatine Journal*, January 21, 1970.

189. Ibid.

190. Weiershauser, "Youthful Administrator."

191. "Reformatory Patient Costs Up in '68; Population Down," *Fort Dodge Messenger*, September 23, 1969.

192. Weiershauser, "Youthful Administrator."

193. Ibid.

194. "May Phase Out R.C. Reformatory," *Fort Dodge Messenger*, May 3, 1969.

195. Frances Craig, "Women 'Growing' in Crime; Is It a Kind of Women's Lib?" *Des Moines Register*, October 22, 1970.

196. Ibid.

197. Ruth Ridge, "Women's Reformatory, Community Churches Sponsor New Venture," *Fort Dodge Messenger*, October 29, 1971.

198. Craig, "Women 'Growing' in Crime."

199. "Name Superintendent," *Muscatine Journal*, December 20, 1972.

200. "Closing Rockwell City," *Des Moines Register*, May 19, 1973.

201. "Reformatory Action in State Legislature," *Rockwell City Advocate*, May 23, 1973.

202. "Inmates Cost State $11,000 Per Year: Audit."

203. Sherry Ricchiardi, "From Prison Life to Cultural Shock," *Des Moines Sunday Register*, October 28, 1973.

204. Ibid.

205. Sherry Ricchiardi, "New Volunteer Program Aids Women Released from Prison," *Des Moines Sunday Register*, March 10, 1974.

206. Steven Walters, "Alternate Proposal for Iowa Prisons," *Des Moines Tribune*, February 4, 1976.

207. John Carlson, "Opposition Voiced to Plan Involving RC Reformatory," *Fort Dodge Messenger*, February 5, 1976.

208. Susan Caba, "Blue-Ribbon Panel to Probe Iowa Prison System Plan," *Fort Dodge Messenger*, October 11, 1976.

209. Sherry Ricchiardi, "Motherhood Doesn't Stop at the Prison Gate," *Des Moines Sunday Register*, May 9, 1976.

210. Ibid.

211. Bob Kenyon, "Women's Reformatory Installs Equipment for Shift Factory," *Fort Dodge Messenger*, July 10, 1976.

212. "Killing Legal at Reformatory, as Long as It's Done with a Book," *Fort Dodge Messenger*, February 17, 1977.

213. M.G. Mooney, "High School Equivalency Program Proves Value of Rehabilitation," *Fort Dodge Messenger*, November 27, 1976.

214. Rans, et al., *Population Profiles*.

215. Lisa Berger, "Profile of the Woman Criminal," *Independent Press-Telegram* (Long Beach, CA), July 24, 1977.

216. Bonnie Wittenburg, "At Least 35 Iowa Escapees are Still Free," *Des Moines Sunday Register*, November 6, 1977.

217. Connie Stewart, "And in Prison," *Des Moines Register*, October 16, 1977.

218. David Yepsen, "Sex, Drug Misconduct at Women's Reformatory Cited," *Des Moines Register*, December 20, 1977.
219. "Stiffer Security, but Inmates Still Attend Classes Unsupervised," *Des Moines Register*, December 21, 1977.
220. Ibid.
221. "Investigation Clears Officials at Reformatory," *Fort Dodge Messenger*, January 16, 1978.
222. Ruth Hall, "Inmate Files Alienation Suit," *Fort Dodge Messenger*, February 9, 1978.
223. Citizens' Aide, *Report to the Governor of Iowa and the Sixty-Seventh General Assembly Second Session* (1978), https://www.ncjrs.gov/pdffiles1/Digitization/46258NCJRS.pdf.
224. Ibid.
225. Bob Brown, "Find No Racial Bias at RC Reformatory," *Fort Dodge Messenger*, December 7, 1977.
226. Margaret Engel, "Ratings System for Prisoners is Criticized," *Des Moines Register*, July 22, 1977.
227. Helen Weiershauser, "Murder, Suffering, Imprisonment—Realities to Sharon Ballenger Finding Different Life," *Muscatine Journal*, March 10, 1978.
228. "Women's Reformatory Supt. Wallman Resigns," *Rockwell City Advocate*, October 25, 1979.
229. "17,500-plus Salaries Paid by State Agencies," *Des Moines Register*, March 29, 1978.
230. "Susan Hunter Will Head Reformatory," *Fort Dodge Messenger*, June 1980.
231. Sherry Ricchiardi, "Women's Reformatory: 'Asking for Trouble,'" *Des Moines Sunday Register*, September 21, 1980; Dennis Freiheit, "Life 'On the Inside,'" *Fort Dodge Messenger*, November 8, 1980.
232. Ricchiardi, "Women's Reformatory."
233. Ibid.
234. "Suit Filed to Increase Women's Reformatory Aid," *Fort Dodge Messenger*, November 26, 1980.
235. David Yepsen, "Rockwell City Reformatory Closing Eyed," *Des Moines Register*, March 23, 1981.
236. Kevin Murphy, "Move of Women's Reformatory All but Settled," *Fort Dodge Messenger*, April 6, 1982.

Chapter 5

237. Marilyn Musser, Dick Brown and Dewey Knudson, "Prison Switch Angers Residents," *Des Moines Tribune*, November 30, 1981; Diane Graham, "Moving of Women Inmates to Mitchellville Backed," *Des Moines Register*, March 3, 1982; Kevin Murphy, "Little Time to Be Wasted in Transfer of R.C. Prisoners," *Fort Dodge Messenger*, May 5, 1982; Offender Account of Transition from Rockwell City to Mitchellville, 1982.

238. Offender Account of Transition.

239. Helen Weiershauser, "Prison Offers Schooling, Crafts, and Library," *Muscatine Journal*, November 16, 1984.

240. Helen Weiershauser, "Women in Prison—A New Series," *Muscatine Journal*, November 10, 1984; Helen Weiershauser, "Inmates Call Her Susan," *Muscatine Journal*, November 12, 1984.

241. Weiershauser, "Inmates Call Her Susan."

242. Weiershauser, "Women in Prison"; Weiershauser, "Inmates Call Her Susan."

243. Helen Weiershausher, "We Have No Guards," *Muscatine Journal*, November 14, 1984; Weiershauser, "Prison Offers Schooling."

244. "We Have No Guards."

245. Helen Weiershausher, "Unit 5 Means Medium Security," *Muscatine Journal*, November 14, 1984.

246. "Lawyers Seek Review of Plan for Grievances," *Des Moines Register*, January 9, 1991.

247. Lou Ortiz, "Little Aid Seen for Drug-using Female Inmates," *Des Moines Register*, August 2, 1989.

248. Kellye Carter, "Program Lets Prisoners Build Skills," *Des Moines Register*, August 2, 1989.

249. "Mitchellville Officials, Citizens Debate Prison Addition at Last-minute Meeting," *Altoona Herald-Mitchellville Index*, March 21, 1991.

250. William Petroski, "Few Fear a Larger Women's Prison," *Des Moines Register*, April 13, 2007.

251. William Petroski, "Tentative OK for Expanded Prison Plans," *Des Moines Register*, June 8, 1990.

252. Bonnie J. Campbell, "Statement of Bonnie J. Campbell. Iowa Correctional Institution for Women," September 18, 1991.

253. Margaret Ludington, "Former Prisoners Say Mitchellville Left Them Unready for the Outside," *Altoona Herald-Mitchellville Index*, April 1992.

254. Barbara Breeding, "If I Get Out," *Des Moines Skywalker*, May 13, 1992.

255. Barbara Breeding, "Match-2 Program Finds Friends for Inmates," *Des Moines Skywalker*, May 27, 1992.

256. Luthern Social Service of Iowa, "Storybook Project Brings Mothers and Children Closer," *News* 59, no. 4 (1999): 1; Meredith Daggett, "Story Project Helps Moms Stay Close to Their Children," *Des Moines Register*, July 28, 1999.

257. Dan Eggen, "Jail Work Crews Won't be 'Chain Gangs,'" *Des Moines Register*, July 4, 1995.

258. History.com Editors, "War on Drugs," *History*, December 17, 2019.

259. William Petroski, "Nearly 5,000 Crowd Prisons," *Des Moines Register*, February 9, 1994.

260. History.com Editors, "War on Drugs."

261. William Petroski, "Prison Sees More Women, Violence," *Des Moines Register*, August 19, 1995.

262. State of Iowa Department of Corrections, "Iowa Correctional Institution for Women," *Inside Iowa's DOC* 1, no. 1 (2003): 5.

263. "Iowa Correctional Institution for Women: Trade, Educational Deficiencies Cited," *Waterloo Courier*, May 16, 1993.

264. State Data Center of Iowa and the Iowa Commission on the State of African-Americans, "African-Americans in Iowa: 2020," State Data Center, February 2020, https://www.iowadatacenter.org.

265. John Shors II, "Systematic Overload," *Des Moines Business Record*, January 13, 1997.

266. Petroski, "Prison Sees More Women."

267. "Iowa to Move Female Inmates to Other States," *Des Moines Register*.

268. William Petroski, "Women's Prison Is Expanded," *Des Moines Register*, May 6, 2000.

269. William Petroski, "Torment, Tumult Persist for Prisoners," *Des Moines Register*, June 2, 2002.

270. Petroski, "Women's Prison Is Expanded"; Diann Wilder-Tomlinson, "Iowa Correctional Institution for Women: 2008 Annual Report," 2008.

271. Abby Simmons, "Group to Honor Lleaders of D.M.'s Black Community," *Des Moines Register*, June 9, 2005.

272. Dawn Sagario, "State Will Help Ex-Inmates Get Jobs," *Des Moines Register*, July 31, 2000; Monee Fields-White, "Firms Turn to Women's Prison for Labor," *Des Moines Register*, November 2, 2000.

273. Lisa Lacher, "Steel Bars and Magnolias," *Drake Alumni News*, Spring 2001.

274. Tammy Conner, "Restoring Relationships Between Mothers, Children," *Newton Daily News*, May 12, 2001.

275. Nancy Dayton, "An Afternoon in Mitchellville," *Gay and Lesbian Resource Center Newsletter*, August 2001; Laurie Mansfield, "Prison Program Opens Doors," *Des Moines Register*, October 31, 2001.

276. "Daily Bulletin," March 13, 2001.

277. Kate Kompas, "A New Leash on Life," *Des Moines Register*, February 11, 2002.

278. William Petroski, "Few Fear a Larger Women's Prison," *Des Moines Register*, April 13, 2007.

279. William Petroski, "Financing for New Prisons Mulled," *Des Moines Register*, January 9, 2009.

280. Patti Wachtendorf, "Iowa Correctional Institution for Women 2016 Annual Report," 2016.

281. Office of the Governor of Iowa, "Voting Rights Restoration," last modified August 5, 2020. https://governor.iowa.gov.

282. Danielle Douglas-Gabriel, "Education Dept. Expands Pell Grant Initiative for Inmates to Take College Classes," *Washington Post*, April 24, 2020.

283. Joseph Shapiro, "In Iowa, a Commitment to Make Prison Work Better for Women," NPR, October 17, 2018.

INDEX

W

ABOUT THE AUTHOR

Photo by Dylan Heuer.

Erica Spiller studied English and theatre arts at Virginia Commonwealth University and Simpson College. She is a two-time winner of Tallgrass Theatre Company's Iowa Playwrights Workshop for her plays *A Light that Burns* and *Again and Again, and Eventually.* Some of her other published works include "(M)other Dracula and Its Adaptations," "Currency of the Body and Mind: A Quest for Agency in the *Memoirs of Laetitia Pilkington*" and "Collaboration of Feminist and Postcolonial Discourses in the Plays of Aphra Behn and Caryl Churchill." Erica was raised in central Iowa, where she currently works in higher education, writes and volunteers as a resident lighting designer at a local theater company. She enjoys spending time with her wife, Lauren; their children, Camden and Austen; and the family's rescue dogs, Scout and Darcy.

Visit us at
www.historypress.com